# Piedmont Community Tree Guide: Benefits, Costs, and Strategic Planting

November 2006

E. Gregory McPherson[1]
James R. Simpson[1]
Paula J. Peper[1]
Shelley L. Gardner[1]
Kelaine E. Vargas[1]
Scott E. Maco[1]
Qingfu Xiao[2]

[1]Center for Urban Forest Research
USDA Forest Service
Pacific Southwest Research Station
Davis, CA

[2]Department of Land, Air, and Water Resources
University of California, Davis

## Contributing Organizations

Center for Urban Forest Research
USDA Forest Service, Pacific Southwest Research Station
Davis, CA

Department of Land, Air, and Water Resources
University of California
Davis, CA

## Sponsoring Organization

USDA Forest Service
State and Private Forestry
Urban and Community Forestry Program

## Acknowledgements

We appreciate the technical assistance provided by Don McSween and Craig Monroe (Charlotte City Engineering, Landscape Management); Greg Ina, Jim Jenkins, and Karen Wise (Davey Resource Group); Ilya Bezdezhskiy, Annalis Zundel, Irene Sheynis, and Stephanie Huang (CUFR).

Tree care expenditure information was provided by Marcia Bansley of Trees Atlanta (Atlanta, GA), Ray Betz of Davey Tree Expert Company (Charlotte, NC), Gene Hyde (City of Chattanooga, TN), Scott Jones (City of Columbus, GA), Karl Pokorny (City of Richmond, VA), Robert Swanson of Caldwell Tree Care (Roswell, GA), and Greg Wallace (Forsyth County, GA).

Donald Ham (The Laurus Group, LLC), Dudley Hartel (USDA Forest Service, Southern Center for Urban Forestry Research and Information), and Nancy Stairs (NC Department of Environment and Natural Resources, Division of Forest Resources) provided helpful reviews of this work.

Mark Buscaino and Ed Macie (USDA Forest Service, State and Private Forestry) provided invaluable support for this project.

# What's in this Tree Guide?

This tree guide is organized as follows:

**Executive Summary**: Presents key findings.

**Chapter 1**: Describes the Guide's purpose, audience, and geographic scope.

**Chapter 2**: Provides background information on the potential of trees in Piedmont communities to provide benefits, and describes management costs that are typically incurred.

**Chapter 3**: Provides calculations of tree benefits and costs for the Piedmont region.

**Chapter 4**: Illustrates how to estimate urban forest benefits and costs for tree planting projects in your community and tips to increase cost-effectiveness.

**Chapter 5**: Presents guidelines for selecting and placing trees in residential yards and public open spaces.

**Appendix A**: Contains tables that list annual benefits and costs of representative tree species at 5-year intervals for 40 years after planting.

**Appendix B**: Describes the methods, assumptions, and limitations associated with estimating tree benefits.

**Glossary of terms**: Provides definitions for technical terms used in the report.

**References**: Lists references cited in the guide.

This guide will help users quantify the long-term benefits and costs associated with proposed tree planting projects. It is available online at http://cufr.ucdavis.edu/products.

The Center for Urban Forest Research (CUFR) has developed a computer program called STRATUM to estimate these values for existing street and park trees. STRATUM is part of the i-Tree software suite. More information on i-Tree and STRATUM is available at www.itreetools.org and the CUFR web site.

# Table of Contents

*The green infrastructure is a significant component of communities in the Piedmont region.*

# *Executive Summary*

This report quantifies benefits and costs for small, medium, and large broadleaf trees and one coniferous tree in the Piedmont region: the species chosen as representative are dogwood (**Cornus florida**), Southern magnolia (**Magnolia grandiflora**), red maple (**Acer rubrum**), and loblolly pine (**Pinus taeda**), respectively. The analysis describes "yard trees (those planted in residential sites) and "public trees" (those planted on streets or in parks). We assume a 55% survival rate over a 40-year time frame. Tree care costs and mortality rates are based on results from a survey of municipal and commercial arborists. Benefits are calculated using tree growth curves and numerical models that consider regional climate, building characteristics, air pollutant concentrations, and prices.

*Benefits and costs quantified*

The measurements used in modeling environmental and other benefits of trees are based on in-depth research carried out for Charlotte, North Carolina. Given the Piedmont region's large and diverse geographical area, this approach provides first-order approximations. It is a general accounting that can be easily adapted and adjusted for local planting projects. Two examples are provided that illustrate how to adjust benefits and costs to reflect different aspects of local planting projects.

*Adjusting values for local planting projects*

Large trees provide the most benefits. Average annual benefits increase with mature tree size:

*Annual benefits*

- $31 to $36 for a small tree

- $41 to $53 for a medium tree

- $103 to $112 for a large tree

- $47 to $60 for a conifer

Benefits associated with reducing stormwater runoff and increasing property value account for the largest proportion of total benefits in this region. Decreased energy use, lower levels of air pollutants and reduced levels of carbon dioxide in the air are the next most important benefits.

Energy conservation benefits vary with tree location as well as size. Trees located opposite west-facing walls provide the greatest net heating and cooling energy savings. Reducing heating and cooling energy needs reduces carbon dioxide emissions and thereby reduces atmospheric carbon dioxide. Similarly, energy savings that reduce pollutant emissions at power plants account for important reductions in gases that produce ozone, a major component of smog.

*Costs*

The average annual costs over 40 years for tree care range from $8 to $36 per tree. (Values below are for yard and public trees, respectively.)

- $18 and $24 for a small tree
- $18 and $24 for a medium tree
- $19 and $27 for a large tree
- $16 and $25 for a conifer

Planting is the greatest cost for trees (annualized to $6 to $13 per tree per year). With the exception of conifers, which require little pruning, tree pruning is the next highest expense ($2 to $8 per tree per year). The costs for the medium and small trees are approximately the same because for the first part of their lives they grow at approximately the same rate and are approximately the same size.

*Average annual net benefits*

Average annual net benefits (benefits minus costs) per tree for a 40-year period are as follows:

- $7 to $18 for a small tree
- $23 to $35 for a medium tree
- $83 to $92 for a large tree
- $31 to $44 for a conifer

Environmental benefits alone, including energy savings, stormwater-runoff reduction, improved air quality, and reduced atmospheric carbon dioxide, are up to three times greater than tree care costs.

*Net benefits summed for 40 years*

Net benefits for a yard tree opposite a west wall and a public tree are substantial when summed over the entire 40-year period (values below are for yard and public trees, respectively):

- $720 and $280 for a small tree
- $1,400 and $960 for a medium tree
- $3,680 and $3,160 for a large tree
- $1,760 and $1,120 for a conifer

Yard trees produce higher net benefits than public trees, primarily because of lower maintenance costs.

*Adjusting for local planting projects*

In order to demonstrate ways in which communities can adapt the information in this report to their needs, two fictional cities interested in increasing their urban forest are created. The benefits and costs of different planting projects are determined. In the hypothetical city of Wild Ramp, net benefits and benefit–cost ratios (BCRs) are calculated for a planting of 1,000 trees (1-inch) assuming a cost of $160 per tree, 55% survival rate, and 40-year analysis. Total costs are $970,000, benefits total $3.6 million, and net benefits are $2.7 million ($66 per tree per year). The BCR is 3.74:1, indicating that $3.74 is returned for every $1 invested. The net benefits and BCRs by mature tree size are:

- $19,500 (1.43:1) for 50 small flowering dogwood trees

- $168,650 (2.26:1) for 150 medium Southern magnolia trees

- $2.3 million (4.35:1) for 700 large red maple trees

- $129,000 (2.42:1) for 100 loblolly pine trees

Hydrology (45%) and increased property values (37%) account for more than three-quarters of the estimated benefits. Reduced energy costs (14%), atmospheric $CO_2$ reduction (3%), and improved air quality (1%) make up the remaining benefits.

In the fictional city of Bassville, long-term planting and tree care costs and benefits were compared to determine if a proposed policy that favors planting small trees would be cost-effective compared to the current policy of planting large trees where space permits. Over a 40-year period, the net benefits would be:

- $257 per tree for a dogwood

- $938 per tree for a Southern magnolia

- $3,166 per tree for a red maple

Based on this analysis, the city of Bassville decided to retain their policy. They now require tree shade plans that show how developers will achieve 50% shade over streets, sidewalks, and parking lots within 15 years of development.

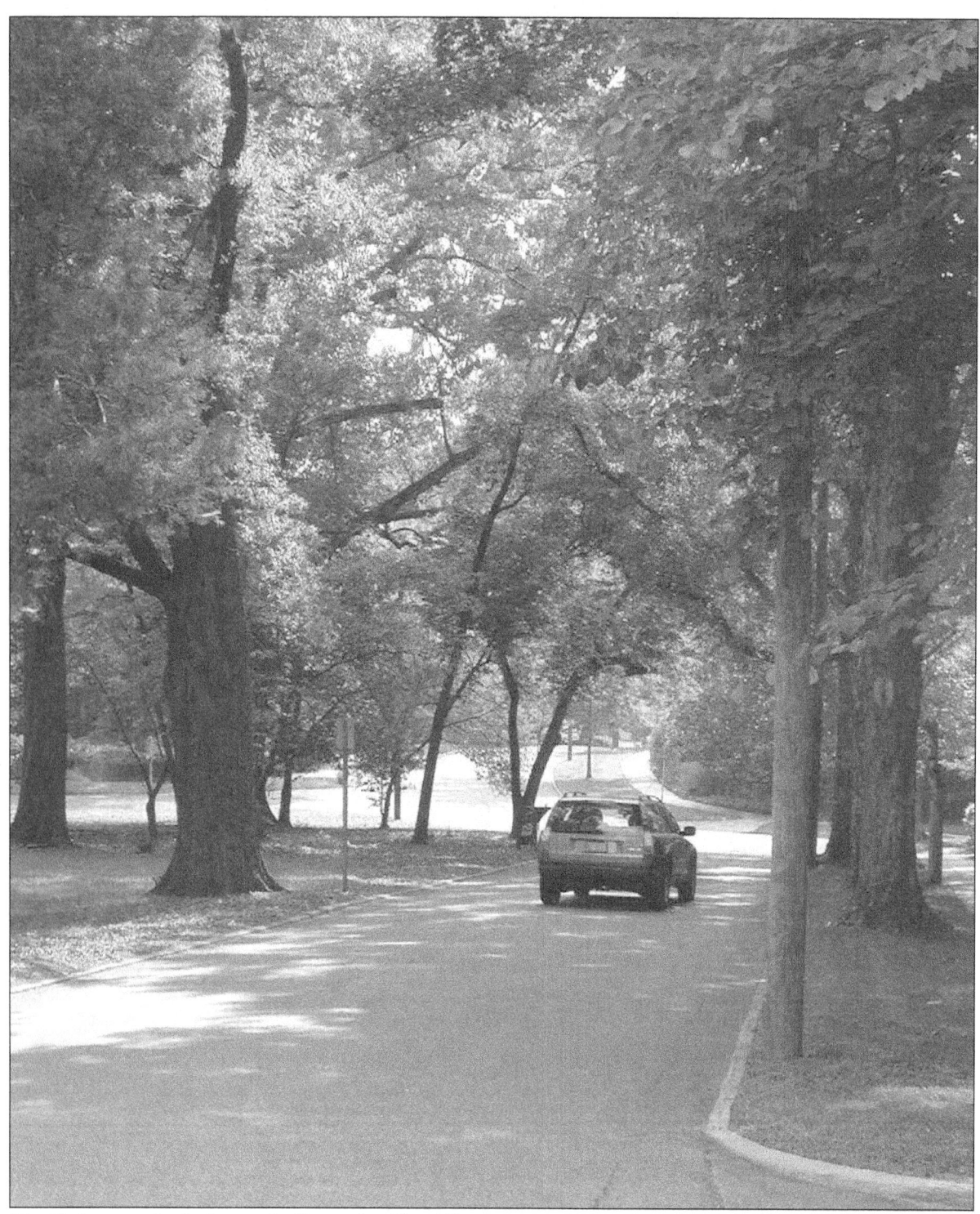

*The Piedmont region is characterized by gently rolling hills, numerous rivers and streams, and a dense, diverse tree cover.*

# Chapter 1. Introduction

From small towns surrounded by cropland or forests to the large metropolitan cities of Charlotte, Atlanta, Washington DC, and Philadelphia, the Piedmont region (**Figure 1**) contains a diverse assemblage of communities. With technology, pharmaceutical research and financial industries joining the traditional economies of agriculture, livestock, and forestry the region is experiencing rapid change. The Piedmont region is home to approximately 35 million people and includes some of the fastest growing cities and counties in the United States.

*Piedmont communities can derive many benefits from community trees*

The word "Piedmont" comes from the French for "foot of the mountain"; the region is characterized by rolling wooded hills separated by rivers and streams. In many places the land has been converted to agriculture and commercial forestry. Lakes, streams, and wetlands are abundant. Forests at the interface of development continue to be an important component of the region's economic, physical and social fabric.

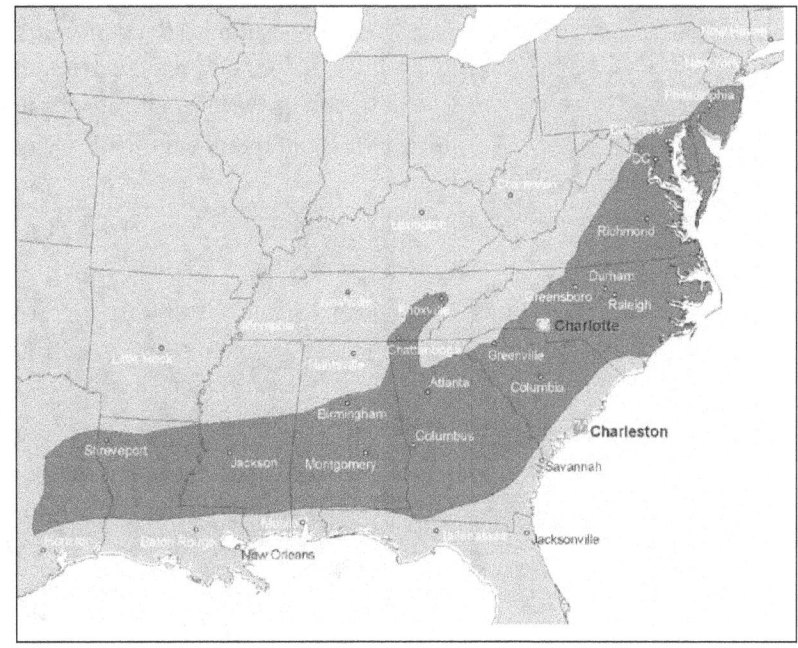

*Figure 1. The Piedmont region (shaded area) extends from southern New Jersey in a broad band south and west to eastern Texas. Charlotte, North Carolina is the reference city for this region.*

Piedmont communities have been surrounded by forests for generations. Only with the recent rapid loss of forest cover associated with urbanization have many residents realized that they were taking these forests for granted. Now there is a sense of urgency to protect what remains, to restore what can be reclaimed, and to create new urban forests that offset the impacts of development.

The Piedmont Region extends in a wide band from southern New Jersey through the heart of Virginia, North and South Carolina, Georgia, Alabama, Mississippi, and Louisiana. Its western and southern extreme is in eastern Texas (**Figure 1**). Boundaries correspond with Sunset Climate Zones 31 and 32 (Brenzel 2001) and USDA Hardiness Zones 6–8. The **climate\*** in this region is mild in the winter, allowing a great number of tree species to thrive. Summers are hot and humid. Annual precipitation ranges from 40 to 60 inches (1,000–1,500 mm).

*\*Bold-faced words are defined in the Glossary.*

In the Piedmont region, urban forest canopies form living umbrellas. They are distinctive features of the landscape that protect us from the elements, clean the water we drink and the air we breathe, and form a living connection to earlier generations who planted and tended these trees.

*Quality of life improves with trees*

As the communities of the Piedmont continue to grow during the coming decades, sustaining healthy **community forests** is integral to the quality of life residents experience. The role of urban forests in enhancing the environment, increasing community attractiveness and livability, and fostering civic pride takes on greater significance as communities strive to balance economic growth with environmental quality and social well-being. The simple act of planting trees provides opportunities to connect residents with nature and with each other. Neighborhood tree plantings and stewardship projects stimulate investment by local citizens, businesses, and governments for the betterment of their communities (**Figure 2**).

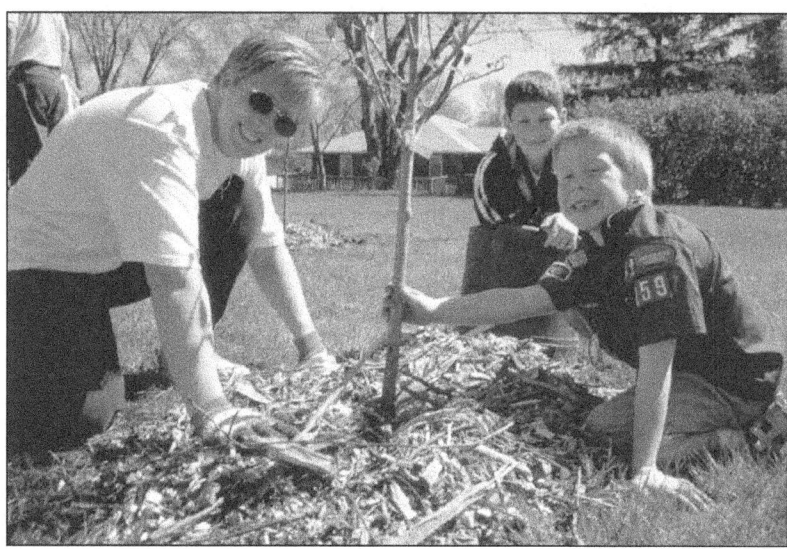

*Figure 2. Tree planting and stewardship programs provide opportunities for local residents to work together to build better communities.*

Community forests bring opportunity for economic renewal, combating development woes, and increasing the quality of life for community residents.

*Trees provide environmental benefits*

Piedmont communities can promote energy efficiency through tree planting and stewardship programs that strategically locate trees to save energy and minimize conflicts with urban infrastructure. The same trees can provide additional benefits by reducing stormwater runoff; improving local air, soil, and water quality; reducing atmospheric carbon dioxide ($CO_2$); providing wildlife habitat; increasing property values; slowing traffic; enhancing community attractiveness and investment; and promoting human well-being.

This guide builds upon previous studies by the U.S. Forest Service in Chicago and Sacramento (McPherson 1998, McPherson et al. 1994), American Forest's urban ecosystem analyses in Atlanta, Washington D.C., Roanoke, Virginia, Mecklenburg County, North Carolina, Montgomery, Alabama (American Forests 2002 a, b, c, 2003, 2004, 2004, respectively), and other regional Tree Guides (McPherson et al. 1999a, 2000, 2003, 2005a) to extend existing knowledge of urban forest benefits in the Piedmont. The guide:

*Scope defined*

- Quantifies benefits of trees on a per-tree basis rather than on a **canopy-cover** basis (it should not be used to estimate benefits for trees growing in forest stands).

- Describes management costs and benefits.

- Details benefits and costs for trees in residential yards and along streets and in parks.

- Illustrates how to use this information to estimate benefits and costs for local tree planting projects.

These guidelines are specific to the Piedmont, and based on measurements and calculations from open-growing urban trees in this region.

Street, park, and shade trees are components of all Piedmont communities, and they impact every resident. Their benefits are myriad. However, with municipal tree programs dependent on taxpayer-supported general funds, communities are forced to ask whether trees are worth the price to plant and care for over the long term, thus requiring urban forestry programs to demonstrate their cost-effectiveness (McPherson 1995). If tree plantings are proven to benefit communities, then monetary commitment to tree programs will be justified. Therefore, the objective of this tree guide is to identify and describe the benefits and costs of planting trees in Piedmont communities—providing a tool for municipal tree managers, arborists, and tree enthusiasts to increase public awareness and support for trees (Dwyer and Miller 1999).

*Audience and objective*

This tree guide addresses a number of questions about the environmental and aesthetic benefits of community tree plantings in Piedmont communities:

*What will this tree guide do?*

- How can tree-planting programs improve environmental quality, conserve energy, and add value to communities?

- Where should residential yard and public trees be placed to maximize their benefits and cost-effectiveness?

- How can conflicts between trees and power lines, sidewalks, and buildings be minimized?

*Trees in Piedmont communities enhance quality of life.*

# Chapter 2. Identifying Benefits and Costs of Urban and Community Forests

This chapter describes benefits and costs of public and privately managed trees. The functional benefits and associated economic value of community forests are described. Expenditures related to tree care and management are assessed—a necessary process for creating cost-effective programs (Hudson 1983, Dwyer et al. 1992).

## *Benefits*

### *Saving Energy*

Energy is an essential ingredient for quality of life and for economic growth. Conserving energy by greening our cities is often more cost-effective than building new power plants. For example, while California was experiencing energy shortages in 2001, its 177 million city trees were providing shade and conserving energy. Annual savings to utilities was an estimated $500 million in wholesale electricity and generation purchases (McPherson and Simpson 2003). Planting 50 million more shade trees in strategic locations would provide savings equivalent to seven 100-megawatt power plants. The cost of peak load reduction was $63/kW, considerably less than the $150/kW benchmark for cost-effectiveness. Like electric utilities throughout the country, utilities in the Piedmont could invest in shade tree programs as a cost-effective energy conservation measure.

*How trees work to save energy*

Trees modify climate and conserve building energy use in three principal ways (**Figure 3**):

- Shading reduces the amount of heat absorbed and stored by built surfaces.

- **Evapotranspiration** converts liquid water to water vapor and thus cools the air by using solar energy that would otherwise result in heating of the air.

- Wind-speed reduction reduces the infiltration of outside air into interior

*Figure 3. Trees save energy for heating and cooling by shading buildings, lowering summertime temperatures, and reducing wind speeds. Secondary benefits from energy conservation are reduced water consumption and reduced pollutant emissions by power plants (drawing by Mike Thomas).*

spaces and reduces heat loss, especially where conductivity is relatively high (e.g., glass windows) (Simpson 1998).

*Trees lower temperatures*

Trees and other vegetation on individual building sites may lower air temperatures 5°F (3°C) compared with outside the **greenspace**. At larger scales (6 square miles [10 km²]), temperature differences of more than 9°F (5°C) have been observed between city centers and more vegetated suburban areas (Akbari et al. 1992). These "hot spots" in cities are called **urban heat island**s.

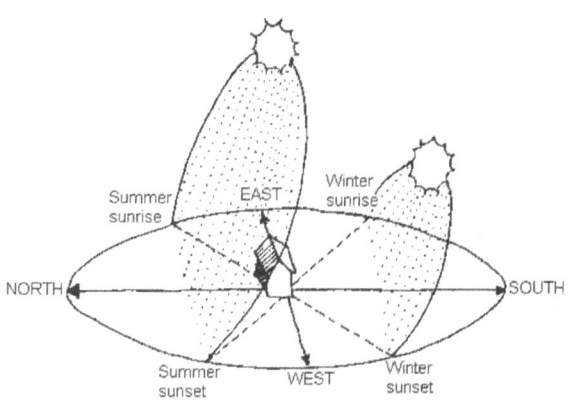

*Figure 4. Paths of the sun on winter and summer solstices (from Sand 1991). Summer heat gain is primarily through east- and west-facing windows and walls. The roof receives most irradiance, but insulated attics reduce heat gain to living spaces. The winter sun, at a lower angle, strikes the south-facing surfaces.*

For individual buildings, strategically placed trees can increase energy efficiency in the summer and winter. Because the summer sun is low in the east and west for several hours each day, solar angles should be considered. Trees that shade east, and especially, west walls help keep buildings cool (**Figure 4**). In the winter, allowing the sun to strike the southern side of a building can warm interior spaces. However, the trunks and bare branches of **deciduous** trees that shade south- and east-facing walls during winter may increase heating costs by blocking 40% or more of winter irradiance (McPherson 1984).

*Windbreaks reduce heat loss*

Rates at which outside air infiltrates a building can increase substantially with wind speed. In cold, windy weather, the entire volume of air, even in newer or tightly sealed homes, may change every two to three hours. Windbreaks reduce wind speed and resulting air infiltration by up to 50%, translating into potential annual heating savings of 10–12% (Heisler 1986). Reductions in wind speed reduce heat transfer through conductive materials as well. Cool winter winds, blowing against windows, can contribute significantly to the heating load of buildings by increasing the temperature gradient between inside and outside temperatures. Windbreaks reduce air infiltration and conductive heat loss from buildings.

*Trees can save money*

Trees provide greater energy savings in the Piedmont than in cooler climate regions because they reduce air conditioning loads during the hot and humid summers. For example, in Atlanta trees were found to produce substantial cooling savings for an energy efficient two-story wood-frame house (McPherson et al. 1993). A computer simulation of annual cooling savings indicated that the typical household with air conditioning spent about $225 each year for cooling. Shade and lower air temperatures from three 25-ft tall (7.5 m) trees—two on the west side of the house and one on the east—were estimated to save $77 each year for cooling, a 34% reduction (1,035 kWh). Conserving energy by greening our cities is important because it can be more cost-effective than building new power plants (see http://www.fs.fed.us/psw/programs/cufr/products/3/cufr_148.pdf). In the Piedmont region, there is ample opportunity to "retrofit" communities with more sustainable landscapes through strategic tree planting and care of existing trees.

*Retrofit for more savings*

## Reducing Atmospheric Carbon Dioxide

Global temperatures have increased since the late 19th century, with major warming periods from 1910 to 1945 and from 1976 to the present (IPCC 2001). Human activities, primarily fossil-fuel consumption, are adding greenhouse gases to the atmosphere, and current research suggests that the recent increases in temperature can be attributed in large part to increases in greenhouse gases (IPCC 2001). Higher global temperatures are expected to have a number of adverse effects, including melting polar ice caps which could raise sea level by 6–37 in (15–94 cm) (Hamburg et al. 1997). With more than one-third of the world's population living in coastal areas (Cohen et al. 1997), the effects could be disastrous. Increasing frequency and duration of extreme weather events will continue to tax emergency management resources. Some plants and animals may become extinct as habitat becomes restricted.

Urban forests have been recognized as important storage sites for carbon dioxide ($CO_2$), the primary greenhouse gas (Nowak and Crane 2002). At the same time, private markets dedicated to reducing $CO_2$ emissions by trading carbon credits are emerging (McHale 2003; CO2e.com 2005). Carbon credits are selling for up to $20 (CO2e.com 2005) per **metric tonne** (t), and the social costs of $CO_2$ emissions are estimated to range from $5.45 to 7.64 per t (Fankhauser 1994). For comparison, for every $19 spent on a tree planting project in Arizona 1 t of atmospheric $CO_2$ was reduced (McPherson and Simpson 1999). As carbon trading markets become accredited and prices rise, these markets could provide financing for community forestry programs.

Urban forests can reduce atmospheric $CO_2$ in two ways (**Figure 5**):

*Trees reduce $CO_2$*

- Trees directly sequester $CO_2$ in their stems and leaves while they grow.

- Trees near buildings can reduce the demand for heating and air conditioning, thereby reducing emissions associated with power production.

On the other hand, vehicles, chain saws, chippers, and other equipment release $CO_2$ during the process of planting and maintaining trees. And eventually, all trees die, and most of the $CO_2$ that has accumulated in their structure is released into the atmosphere through decomposition. The rate of release into the atmosphere depends on if and how the wood is reused. For instance, recycling of urban wood waste into products such as furniture can delay the rate of decomposition compared to its reuse as mulch.

*Figure 5. Trees sequester $CO_2$ as they grow and indirectly reduce $CO_2$ emissions from power plants through energy conservation. At the same time, $CO_2$ is released through decomposition and tree care activities that involve fossil-fuel consumption (drawing by Mike Thomas).*

Typically, $CO_2$ released due to tree planting, maintenance, and other program-related activities is about 2–8% of annual $CO_2$ reductions obtained through sequestration and **avoided power plant emissions** (McPherson and Simpson 1999). To provide a complete picture of atmospheric $CO_2$ reductions from tree plantings it is important to consider $CO_2$ released into the atmosphere through tree planting and care activities, as well as decomposition of wood from pruned or dead trees.

*Avoided $CO_2$ emissions*

Regional variations in climate and the mix of fuels that produce energy to heat and cool buildings influence potential $CO_2$ emission reductions. Charlotte, NC's average emission rate is 1,950 lbs (885 kg) $CO_2$/kWh (US EPA 2003). Due to the large amount of coal (43%) in the mix of fuels used to generate the power, this emission rate is higher than in some other regions. For example, the two-state average for Oregon and Washington is much lower, 308 lbs (140 kg) $CO_2$/kWh, because hydroelectric power predominates. The Piedmont region's relatively high $CO_2$ emission rate means greater benefits from reduced energy demand relative to other regions with lower emissions rates.

A study of Chicago's urban forest found that the region's trees stored about 7 million tons (6.4 million t) of atmospheric $CO_2$ (Nowak 1994a). The 51 million trees sequestered approximately 155,000 tons (140,600 t) of atmospheric $CO_2$ annually.

18

Another study in Chicago focused on the carbon sequestration benefit of residential tree **canopy cover**. Tree canopy cover in two residential neighborhoods was estimated to sequester on average 0.112 $lb/ft^2$ (0.547 $kg/m^2$), and pruning activities released 0.016 $lb/ft^2$ (0.08 $kg/m^2$) (Jo and McPherson 1995). Net annual carbon uptake was 0.096 $lb/ft^2$ (0.47 $kg/m^2$).

A comprehensive study of $CO_2$ reduction by Sacramento's urban forest found the region's 6 million trees offset 1.8% of the total $CO_2$ emitted annually as a by-product of human consumption (McPherson 1998). This savings could be substantially increased through strategic planting and long-term stewardship that maximized future energy savings from new tree plantings.

*$CO_2$ reduction through community forestry*

Since 1990, Trees Forever, an Iowa-based non-profit organization, has planted trees for energy savings and atmospheric $CO_2$ reduction with utility sponsorships. Over 1 million trees have been planted in 400 communities with the help of 120,000 volunteers. These trees are estimated to offset $CO_2$ emissions by 50,000 tons (45,359 t) annually. Based on an Iowa State University study, survival rates are an amazing 91% indicating a highly trained and committed volunteer force (Ramsay 2002).

## Improving Air Quality

Approximately 159 million people live in areas where **ozone** ($O_3$) concentrations violate federal air quality standards. About 100 million people live in areas where dust and other small particle matter (**$PM_{10}$**) exceed levels for healthy air. Air pollution is a serious health threat to many city dwellers, causing asthma, coughing, headaches, respiratory and heart disease, and cancer (Smith 1990). Impaired health results in increased social costs for medical care, greater absenteeism, and reduced longevity.

More than half of the counties with severe levels of ozone are in the Piedmont region (US EPA 2005). The most severe are Philadelphia-Wilmington-Trenton, Washington DC, Atlanta, Baltimore, Atlantic City, and Smyth County, VA (US EPA 2005). Tree planting is one practical strategy for communities in these areas to meet and sustain mandated air quality standards.

Recently, the Environmental Protection Agency recognized tree planting as a measure for reducing $O_3$ in State Implementation Plans. Air quality management districts have funded tree planting projects to control particulate matter. These policy decisions are creating new opportunities to plant and care for trees as a method for controlling

*The EPA recognizes that trees improve air quality*

air pollution (Luley and Bond 2002, for more information see www.treescleanair.org).

Urban forests provide five main air quality benefits (**Figure 6**):

- They absorb gaseous pollutants (e.g., ozone, **nitrogen dioxide [NO$_2$]**, and **sulfur dioxide [SO$_2$]**) through leaf surfaces.

- They intercept small particulate matter (**PM$_{10}$**) (e.g., dust, ash, pollen, smoke).

- They release oxygen through **photosynthesis**.

- They transpire water and shade surfaces, which lowers air temperatures, thereby reducing ozone levels.

- They reduce energy use, which reduces emissions of pollutants from power plants, including NO$_2$, SO$_2$ PM$_{10}$, and volatile organic compounds (**VOC**s).

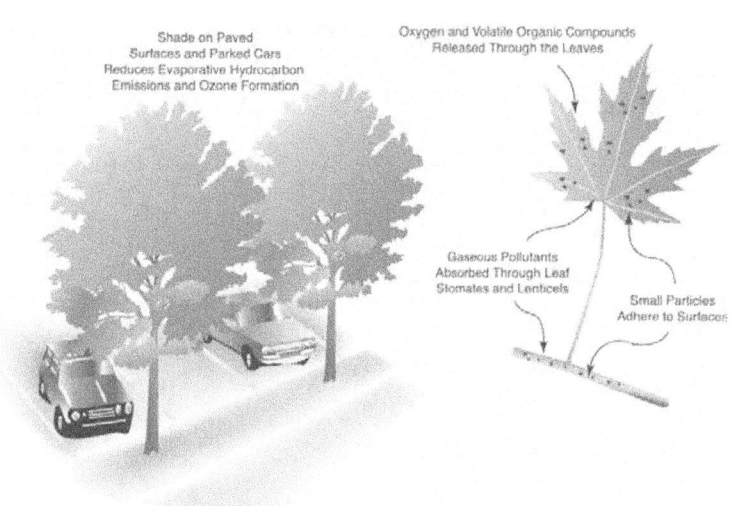

Figure 6. Trees absorb gaseous pollutants, retain particles on their surfaces, and release oxygen and volatile organic compounds. By cooling urban heat islands and shading parked cars, trees can reduce ozone formation (drawing by Mike Thomas).

Trees can adversely affect air quality. Most trees emit **biogenic volatile organic compounds** (BVOCs) such as isoprenes and monoterpenes that can contribute to O$_3$ formation. The contribution of BVOC emissions from city trees to O$_3$ formation depends on complex geographic and atmospheric interactions that have not been studied in most cities. Some complicating factors include variations with temperature and atmospheric levels of NO$_2$. As well, the ozone-forming potential of different tree species varies considerably (Benjamin and Winer 1998). Genera having the greatest relative effect on increasing O$_3$ are sweetgum (**Liquidambar** spp.), black gum (**Nyssa** spp.), sycamore (**Platanus** spp.), poplar (**Populus** spp.), and oak (**Quercus** spp.) (Nowak 2000). A computer simulation study for Atlanta found that it would be very difficult to meet EPA ozone standards using trees because of the high BVOC emissions from pines and other vegetation (Chameides et al. 1988). In the Los Angeles basin, increased planting of low BVOC-emitting tree species would reduce O$_3$ concentrations, while planting of medium- and high-emitters would increase overall O$_3$ concentrations (Taha 1996). A study in the northeastern United States, however, found that species mix had no detectable effects on

$O_3$ concentrations (Nowak et al. 2000). These potentially negative effects of trees on one kind of air pollution must be considered in light of their great benefit in other areas.

Trees absorb gaseous pollutants through leaf stomates—tiny openings in the leaves. Secondary methods of pollutant removal include adsorption of gases to plant surfaces and uptake through bark pores. Once gases enter the leaf they diffuse into intercellular spaces, where some react with inner leaf surfaces and others are absorbed by water films to form acids. Pollutants can damage plants by altering their metabolism and growth. At high concentrations, pollutants cause visible damage to leaves, such as stippling and bleaching (Costello and Jones 2003). Though they may pose health hazards to plants, pollutants such as nitrogenous gases can be sources of essential nutrients for trees.

*Trees absorb gaseous pollutants*

Trees intercept small airborne particles. Some particles that impact a tree are absorbed, but most adhere to plant surfaces. Species with hairy or rough leaf, twig, and bark surfaces are efficient interceptors (Smith and Dochinger 1976). Intercepted particles are often resuspended to the atmosphere when wind blows the branches, and rain will wash some particulates off plant surfaces. The ultimate fate of these pollutants depends on whether they fall onto paved surfaces and enter the stormwater system, or fall on pervious surfaces, where they are filtered in the soil.

*Trees intercept particulate matter*

Urban forests freshen the air we breathe by releasing oxygen as a by-product of photosynthesis. Net annual oxygen production varies depending on tree species, size, health, and location. A healthy tree, for example, a 32-ft tall (10 m) ash, produces about 260 lb (115 kg) of net oxygen annually (McPherson 1997). A typical person consumes 386 lb (175 kg) of oxygen per year. Therefore, two medium-sized, healthy trees can supply the oxygen required for a single person over the course of a year.

*Trees release oxygen*

Trees near buildings can reduce the demand for heating and air conditioning, thereby reducing emissions of $PM_{10}$, $SO_2$, $NO_2$, and VOCs associated with electric power production. Avoided emissions from trees can be sizable. For example, a strategically located tree can save 100 kWh in electricity for cooling annually (McPherson and Simpson 1999, 2003). Assuming that this conserved electricity comes from a new coal-fired power plant, the tree reduces emissions of $SO_2$ by 0.38 lb (0.17 kg), $NO_2$ by 0.27 lb (0.12 kg), and particulate matter by 0.84 lb (0.38 kg) (US EPA 1989). The same tree is responsible for conserving 60 gal (0.23 m³) of water in cooling towers and reducing $CO_2$ emissions by 200 lb (91 kg).

*Trees save energy, thereby reducing air pollution from power plants*

*Trees effectively reduce ozone and particulate matter concentrations*

In Charlotte, NC, the tree **canopy** (49%) was estimated to remove 3,591 tons (3,257 t) of air pollutants annually with a value of $17.9 million (American Forests 2003). The city of Montgomery, AL's urban forest (33% tree cover) removed 1,603 tons (1,454 t) of air pollutants valued at $7.9 million (American Forests 2004). Chicago's 50.8 million trees were estimated to remove 234 tons (212 t) of $PM_{10}$, 210 tons (191 t) of $O_3$, 93 tons (84 t) of sulfur dioxide ($SO_2$), and 17 tons (15 t) of carbon monoxide in 1991. This environmental service was valued at $9.2 million (Nowak 1994b).

*What about hydrocarbons?*

Trees in a Davis, CA, parking lot were found to improve air quality by reducing air temperatures 1–3°F (0.5–1.5°C) (Scott et al. 1999). By shading asphalt surfaces and parked vehicles, trees reduce hydrocarbon emissions (VOCs) from gasoline that evaporates out of leaky fuel tanks and worn hoses (**Figure 7**). These evaporative emissions are a principal component of smog, and parked vehicles are a primary source. In California, parking lot tree plantings can be funded as an air quality improvement measure because of the associated reductions in evaporative emissions.

*Figure 7. Trees planted to shade parking areas can reduce hydrocarbon emissions and improve air quality.*

### Reducing Stormwater Runoff and Improving Hydrology

*Trees protect water and soil resources*

Urban stormwater runoff is a major source of pollution entering wetlands, streams, lakes, and oceans. Healthy trees can reduce the amount of runoff and pollutants in receiving waters (Cappiella et al. 2005). This is important because federal law requires states and localities to control nonpoint-source pollution, such as runoff from pavements, buildings, and landscapes. Trees are mini-reservoirs, controlling runoff at the source, thereby reducing runoff volumes and erosion of watercourses, as well as delaying the onset of **peak flows**. Trees can reduce runoff in several ways (**Figure 8**):

- Leaves and branch surfaces intercept and store rainfall, thereby reducing runoff volumes and delaying the onset of peak flows.

- Roots increase the rate at which rainfall infiltrates soil and the capacity of soil to store water, reducing overland flow.

- Tree canopies reduce soil erosion by diminishing the impact of raindrops on barren surfaces.

- **Transpiration** through tree leaves reduces soil moisture, increasing the soil's capacity to store rainfall.

Rainfall that is stored temporarily on canopy leaf and bark surfaces is called intercepted rainfall. Intercepted water evaporates, drips from leaf surfaces, and flows down stem surfaces to the ground. **Tree-surface saturation** generally occurs after 1–2 inches (2.5–5 cm) of rainfall has fallen (Xiao and others 2000). During large storm events, rainfall exceeds the amount that the tree **crown** can store, about 50–100 gal (6.7–13.4 m³) per tree. The **interception** benefit is the amount of rainfall that does not reach the ground because it evaporates from the crown. As a result, the volume of runoff is reduced and the time of peak flow is delayed. Trees protect water quality by substantially reducing runoff during small rainfall events that are responsible for most pollutant washoff. Therefore, urban forests generally produce more benefits through water quality protection than through flood control (Xiao et al 1998, 2000).

The amount of rainfall trees intercept depends on their architecture, rainfall patterns, and climate. Tree-crown characteristics that influence interception are the trunk, stem, and surface areas, textures, area of gaps, period when leaves are present, and dimensions (e.g., tree height and diameter). Trees with coarse surfaces retain more rainfall than those with smooth surfaces. Large trees generally intercept more rainfall than small trees do because greater surface areas allow for greater evaporation rates. Tree crowns with few gaps reduce throughfall to the ground.

*Trees reduce runoff*

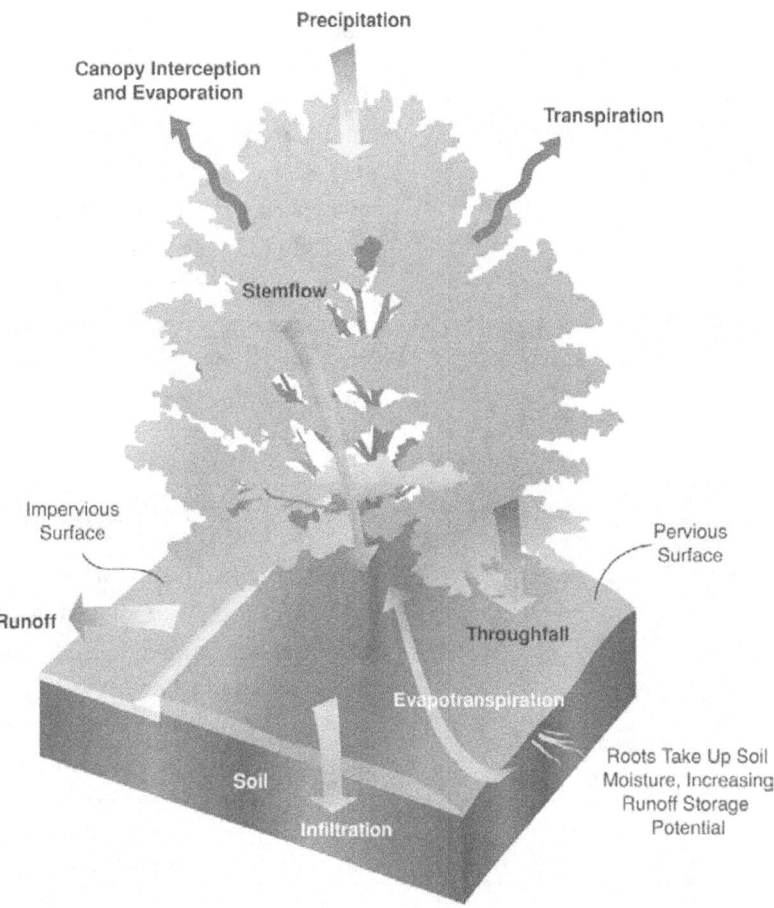

*Figure 8. Trees intercept a portion of rainfall that then evaporates and never reaches the ground. Some rainfall runs to the ground along branches and stems (stemflow) and some falls through gaps or drips off leaves and branches (throughfall). Transpiration increases soil moisture storage potential (drawing by Mike Thomas).*

Species that are in-leaf when rainfall is plentiful are more effective than species that have dropped their leaves during the rainy season.

Studies that have simulated urban forest effects on stormwater runoff have reported reductions of 2 to 7%. Annual interception of rainfall by Sacramento's urban forest for the total urbanized area was only about 2% due to the winter rainfall pattern and lack of **evergreen** species (Xiao et al. 1998). However, average interception under the tree canopy ranged from 6 to 13% (150 gal [0.57 m$^3$] per tree), close to values reported for rural forests. Broadleaf evergreens and **conifers** intercept more rainfall than deciduous species in areas where rainfall is highest in fall, winter, or spring (Xiao and McPherson 2002).

*Value of runoff reduction*

The city of Montgomery, Alabama's tree canopy (34%) reduced runoff by 227 million cubic feet (6.5 million m$^3$), valued at $454 million per 20-year construction cycle (American Forests 2004). In Charlotte, the existing canopy (49%) reduced runoff by 398 million cubic feet (11.3 million m$^3$), with an estimated value of $797 million (American Forests 2003).

*Urban forests can treat wastewater*

Urban forests can provide other hydrologic benefits, too. For example, tree plantations or nurseries can be irrigated with partially treated wastewater. Infiltration of water through the soil can be a safe and productive means of water treatment. Reused wastewater applied to urban forest lands can recharge aquifers, reduce stormwater-treatment loads, and create income through sales of nursery or wood products. Recycling urban wastewater into greenspace areas can be an economical means of treatment and disposal, while at the same time providing other environmental benefits (Natural Resource Conservation Center 2005).

### Aesthetics and Other Benefits

*Beautification*

Trees provide a host of aesthetic, social, economic, and health benefits that should be included in any benefit–cost analysis. One of the most frequently cited reasons that people plant trees is for beautification. Trees add color, texture, line, and form to the landscape. In this way, trees soften the hard geometry that dominates built environments. Research on the aesthetic quality of residential streets has shown that street trees are the single strongest positive influence on scenic quality (Schroeder and Cannon 1983).

*Attractiveness of retail settings*

Consumer surveys have found that preference ratings increase with the presence of trees in the commercial streetscape. In contrast to areas without trees, shoppers shop more often and longer in well-landscaped business districts. They were willing to pay more for parking and up to 11% more for goods and services (Wolf 1999).

Research in public housing complexes found that outdoor spaces with trees were used significantly more often than spaces without trees. By facilitating interactions among residents, trees can contribute to reduced levels of domestic violence, as well as foster safer and more sociable neighborhood environments (Sullivan and Kuo 1996).

*Public safety benefits*

Well-maintained trees increase the "curb appeal" of properties (**Figure 9**). Research comparing sales prices of residential properties with different numbers of trees suggests that people are willing to pay 3–7% more for properties with ample trees versus few or no trees. One of the most comprehensive studies of the influence of trees on residential property values was based on actual sales prices and found that each large front-yard tree was associated with about a 1% increase in sales price (Anderson and Cordell 1988). A much greater value of 9% ($15,000) was determined in a U.S. Tax Court case for the loss of a large black oak on a property valued at $164,500 (Neely 1988). Depending on average home sales prices, the value of this benefit can contribute significantly to cities' property tax revenues.

*Property value benefits*

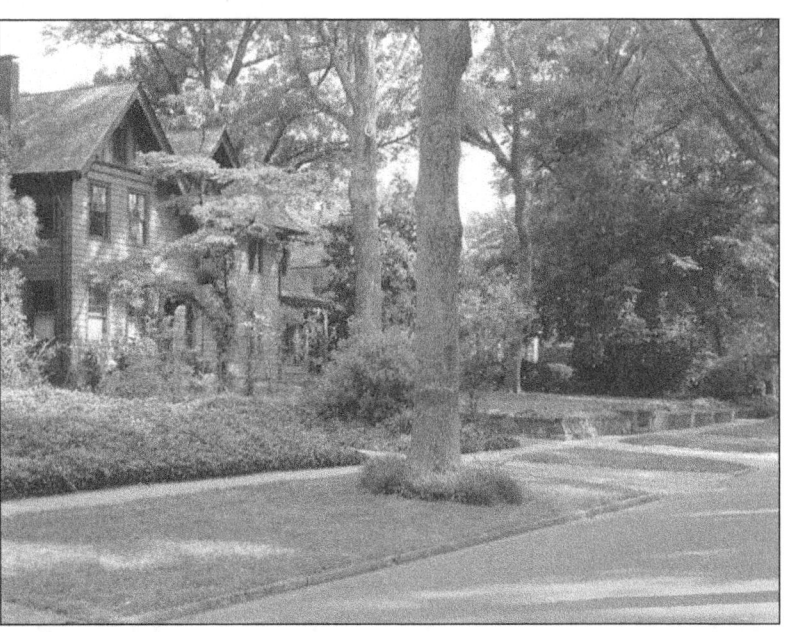

*Figure 9. Trees beautify a neighborhood, increasing property values and creating a more sociable environment.*

Scientific studies confirm our intuition that trees in cities provide social and psychological benefits. Humans derive substantial pleasure from trees, whether it is inspiration from their beauty, a spiritual connection, or a sense of meaning (Dwyer et al. 1992; Lewis 1996). Following natural disasters people often report a sense of loss if their community forest has been damaged (Hull 1992). Views of trees and nature from homes and offices provide restorative experiences that ease mental fatigue and help people to concentrate (Kaplan and Kaplan 1989). Desk-workers with a view of nature report lower rates of sickness and greater satisfaction with their jobs compared to those having no visual connection to nature (Kaplan 1992). Trees provide important settings for recreation and relaxation in and near cities. The act of planting trees can have social value, as bonds between people and local groups often result.

*Social and psychological benefits*

The presence of trees in cities provides public health benefits and improves the well-being of those who live, work, and play in cities. Physical and emotional stress has both short-term and long-term ef-

*Human health benefits*

fects. Prolonged stress can compromise the human immune system. A series of studies on human stress caused by general urban conditions and city driving show that views of nature reduce stress response of both body and mind (Parsons et al. 1998). Urban green also appears to have an "immunization effect," in that people show less stress response if they have had a recent view of trees and vegetation. Hospitalized patients with views of nature and time spent outdoors need less medication, sleep better, have a better outlook, and recover more quickly than patients without connections to nature (Ulrich 1985). Skin cancer is a particular concern in the sunny Piedmont region. Trees reduce exposure to ultraviolet light, thereby lowering the risk of harmful effects from skin cancer and cataracts (Tretheway and Manthe 1999).

*Noise reduction*

Certain environmental benefits from trees are more difficult to quantify than those previously described, but can be just as important. Noise can reach unhealthy levels in cities. Trucks, trains, and planes can produce noise that exceeds 100 decibels, twice the level at which noise becomes a health risk. Thick strips of vegetation in conjunction with landforms or solid barriers can reduce highway noise by 6–15 decibels. Plants absorb more high frequency noise than low frequency, which is advantageous to humans since higher frequencies are most distressing to people (Cook 1978).

*Wildlife habitat*

Numerous types of wildlife inhabit cities and are generally highly valued by residents. For example, older parks, cemeteries, and botanical gardens often contain a rich assemblage of wildlife. Remnant woodlands and **riparian habitats** within cities can connect a city to its surrounding bioregion (**Figure 10**). Wetlands, greenways (linear parks), and other greenspace can provide habitats that conserve **biodiversity** (Platt et al. 1994).

*Figure 10. Natural areas within cities are refuges for wildlife and help connect city dwellers wtith their ecosystems.*

Urban forestry can provide jobs for both skilled and unskilled labor. Public service programs and grassroots-led urban and community forestry programs provide horticultural training to volunteers across the United States. Also, urban and community forestry provides educational opportunities for residents who want to learn about nature through first-hand experience (McPherson and Mathis 1999). Local nonprofit tree groups and municipal volunteer programs

26

often provide educational material and hands-on training in the care of trees and work with area schools.

Tree shade on streets can help offset pavement management costs by protecting paving from weathering. The asphalt paving on streets contains stone aggregate in an oil binder. Tree shade lowers the street surface temperature and reduces heating and volatilization of the binder (McPherson and Muchnick 2005). As a result, the aggregate remains protected for a longer period by the oil binder. When unprotected, vehicles loosen the aggregate, and much like sandpaper, the loose aggregate grinds down the pavement. Because most weathering of asphalt-concrete pavement occurs during the first 5 to 10 years, when new street tree plantings provide little shade, this benefit mainly applies when older streets are resurfaced (**Figure 11**).

*Shade can reduce street maintenance*

*Figure 11. Although shade trees can be expensive to maintain, their shade can reduce the costs of resurfacing streets (McPherson and Muchnick 2005), promote pedestrian travel, and improve air quality directly through pollutant uptake and indirectly through reduced emissions of volatile organic compounds from cars.*

## Costs

### Planting and Maintaining Trees

The environmental, social and economic benefits of urban and community forests come at a price. A national survey reported that communities in the Piedmont region spent an average of about $7.77 per tree, in 1994, for street- and park-tree management (Tschantz and Sacamano 1994) This amount is relatively high, with two national regions spending more than this and eight regions spending less. Nationwide, the single largest expenditure was for tree pruning, followed by tree removal/disposal, and tree planting.

Our survey of **municipal foresters** in Charlotte, NC, Richmond, VA, Cumming, GA, Columbus, GA, and Chattanooga, TN, indicates that

*Cities in the Piedmont spend about $22 per tree*

they are spending about $22 per tree annually. Most of this amount is for pruning ($8 per tree), planting ($6 per tree), removal and disposal ($5 per tree) and administration ($3 per tree). Other municipal departments incur costs for infrastructure repair and trip-and-fall claims that average about $5 per tree annually.

*Tree planting*

Frequently, trees in new residential subdivisions are planted by developers, while cities and counties and volunteer groups plant trees on existing streets and parklands. In some cities, tree planting has not kept pace with removals. Moreover, limited growing space in cities or preferences for flowering trees results in increased planting of smaller, shorter-lived species that provide fewer benefits than larger trees do.

*Residential costs vary*

Annual expenditures for tree management on private property have not been well documented. Costs vary considerably, ranging from some commercial or residential properties that receive regular professional landscape service to others that are virtually "wild" and without maintenance. An analysis of data for Sacramento suggested that households typically spent about $5 to $10 annually per tree for pruning and pest and disease control (McPherson et al. 1993; Summit and McPherson 1998). Our survey of commercial arborists in the Piedmont indicated that expenditures typically range from $15 to $19 per tree. Expenditures are usually greatest for pruning, planting, and removal.

*Irrigation costs*

Due to the region's warm summer climate, newly planted trees may require watering for three to five years. Once established, trees in the Piedmont rarely require additional watering. During drought years, however, a small annual cost may occur.

### Conflicts with Urban Infrastructure

*Tree roots can damage sidewalks*

Like other cities across the United States, communities in the Piedmont region are spending millions of dollars each year to manage conflicts between trees and powerlines, sidewalks, sewers, and other elements of the urban infrastructure. According to the city forester of Charlotte, NC, Charlotte spends an average of $637,000 or about $7 per tree on sidewalk, curb, and gutter repair costs. This amount is less than the $11.22 per tree reported for 18 California cities (McPherson 2000). As well, the figures for California apply only to street trees and do not include repair costs for damaged sewer lines, building foundations, parking lots, and various other **hardscape** elements.

In some Piedmont cities, decreasing budgets are increasing the sidewalk-repair backlog and forcing cities to shift the costs of sidewalk repair to residents. This shift has significant impacts on residents in older areas, where large trees have outgrown small sites and infrastructure has deteriorated. It should be noted that trees should not always bear full reponsibility. In older areas, in particular, sidewalks and curbs may have reached the end of their 20-25 year service life, or been poorly constructed in the first place (Sydnor et al. 2000).

Efforts to control the costs of these conflicts are having alarming effects on urban forests (Bernhardt and Swiecki 1993, Thompson and Ahern 2000):

*Cost of conflicts*

- Cities are downsizing their urban forests by planting smaller trees. Although small trees are appropriate under powerlines and in small planting sites, they are less effective than large trees at providing shade, absorbing air pollutants, and intercepting rainfall.

- Sidewalk damage was the second most common reason that street and park trees were removed. Thousands of healthy urban trees are lost each year and their benefits forgone because of this problem.

- Most cities surveyed were removing more trees than they were planting. Residents forced to pay for sidewalk repairs may not want replacement trees.

Cost-effective strategies to retain benefits from large street trees while reducing costs associated with infrastructure conflicts are described in **Strategies to Reduce Infrastructure Damage by Tree Roots** (Costello and Jones 2003). Matching the growth characteristics of trees to the conditions at the planting site is one important strategy.

Tree roots can also damage old sewer lines that are cracked or otherwise susceptible to invasion. Sewer repair companies estimate that sewer damage is minor until trees and sewers are over 30 years old, and roots from trees in yards are usually more of a problem than roots from trees in planter strips along streets. The latter assertion may be due to the fact that sewers are closer to the root zone as they enter houses than at the street. Repair costs typically range from $100 for sewer roding (inserting a cleaning implement to temporarily remove roots) to $1,000 or more for sewer excavation and replacement.

*Cleaning up after trees*

Most communities sweep their streets regularly to reduce surface-run-off pollution entering local waterways. Street trees drop leaves, flowers, fruit, and branches year round that constitute a significant portion of debris collected from city streets. When leaves fall and winter rains begin, **tree litter** can clog sewers, dry wells, and other elements of flood-control systems. Costs include additional labor needed to remove leaves, and property damage caused by localized flooding. Windstorms also incur clean-up costs. Although serious natural catastrophes are infrequent, they can result in large expenditures.

The cost of addressing conflicts between trees and powerlines is reflected in electric rates. Large trees under power lines require more frequent pruning than better-suited trees, which can make them appear less attractive (**Figure 12**). Frequent crown reduction reduces the benefits these trees could otherwise provide. Moreover, increased costs for pruning are passed on to customers.

*Figure 12. Large trees planted under power lines can require extensive pruning, which increases tree care costs and reduces the benefits of those trees, including their appearance.*

### Wood Salvage, Recycling, and Disposal

According to our survey, most Piedmont cities are recycling green waste from urban trees as mulch, compost, and firewood. Some power plants will use this wood to generate electricity, thereby helping defray costs for hauling and grinding. Generally, the net costs of waste-wood disposal are less than 1% of total tree-care costs, and cities and contractors may break even. Hauling and recycling costs are nearly offset by revenues from sales of mulch, milled lumber and firewood. The cost of wood disposal may be higher depending on geographic location and the presence of exotic pests that require elaborate waste-wood disposal.

# Chapter 3. Determining Benefits and Costs of Community Forests in Piedmont Communities

This chapter presents estimated benefits and costs for trees planted in typical residential yards and public sites. Because benefits and costs vary with tree size, we report results for representative large, medium, and small broadleaf trees and for a representative conifer.

Estimates of benefits and costs are initial approximations as some benefits and costs are intangible or difficult to quantify (e.g., impacts on psychological health, crime, and violence). Limited knowledge about the physical processes at work and their interactions makes estimates imprecise (e.g., fate of air pollutants trapped by trees and then washed to the ground by rainfall). Tree growth and mortality rates are highly variable throughout the region. Benefits and costs also vary, depending on differences in climate, air pollutant concentrations, tree-maintenance practices, and other factors. Given the Piedmont region's large geographical area, with many different climates, soils, and types of community forestry programs, the approach used here provides first-order approximations. It is a general accounting that can be easily adapted and adjusted for local planting projects. It provides a basis for decisions that set priorities and influence management direction (Maco and McPherson 2003).

*Estimates are initial approximations*

## Overview of Procedures

### Approach

In this study, annual benefits and costs are estimated over a 40-year planning horizon for newly planted trees in three residential yard locations (east, south, and west of the residence) and a public street-side or park location (**Appendix A**). Henceforth, we refer to trees in these hypothetical locations as "yard" trees and "public" trees, respectively. Prices are assigned to each cost (e.g., planting, pruning, removal, irrigation, infrastructure repair, liability) and benefit (e.g., heating/cooling energy savings, air pollutant mitigation, stormwater runoff reduction, property value increase) through direct estimation and implied valuation of benefits as environmental externalities. This approach makes it possible to estimate the net benefits of plantings in "typical" locations using "typical" tree species. More information on data collection, modeling procedures, and assumptions can be found in **Appendix B**.

*Benefit and cost estimation*

To account for differences in the mature size and growth of different tree species, we report results for a small (**Cornus florida**, dogwood), medium (**Magnolia grandiflora**, Southern magnolia), and

*Small, medium, and large broadleaf trees and a conifer*

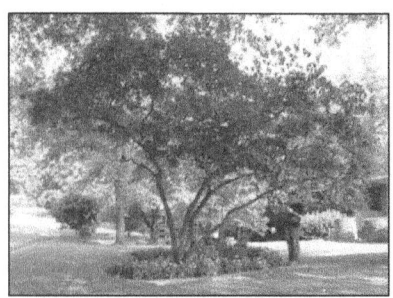

*Figure 13. The flowering dogwood represents small broadleaf trees in this guide.*

large (**Acer rubrum**, red maple) broadleaf tree and a conifer (**Pinus taeda**, loblolly pine) (**Figures 13–16**). Tree dimensions are derived from growth curves developed from street trees in Charlotte, NC (McPherson et al. 2005b).

Frequency and costs of tree management are estimated based on surveys with municipal foresters as described above. In addition, commercial arborists from Roswell, GA, and Charlotte, NC, provided information on tree-management costs on residential properties.

Benefits are calculated with numerical models and input data both from the region (e.g., pollutant emission factors for avoided emissions due to energy savings) and from local sources (e.g., Charlotte climate data for energy effects). Regional electricity and natural gas prices are used in this study to quantify energy savings. Control costs are used to estimate **willingness to pay**. For example, the value of air quality benefits is estimated using marginal control costs (Wang and Santini 1995). If a developer is willing to pay an average of $1 per lb of treated and controlled pollutant to meet minimum standards, then the air-pollution mitigation value of a tree that intercepts 1 lb of pollution, eliminating the need for control, should be $1.

*Tree benefits based on numerical models*

### Reporting Results

*Tree mortality included*

Results are reported in terms of annual value per tree planted. To make these calculations realistic, however, mortality rates are included. Based on our survey of regional municipal foresters and commercial arborists, this analysis assumes that 45% of the planted trees will die over the 40-year period. Annual mortality rates are 2% per year for the first 5 years and 1% per year for the remainder of the 40-year period. This accounting approach "grows" trees in different locations and uses computer simulation to directly calculate the annual flow of benefits and costs as trees mature and die (McPherson 1992). In **Appendix A**, results are reported at 5-year intervals for 40 years.

## Findings of this Study

### Average Annual Net Benefits

Average annual net benefits (benefits minus costs) per tree increase with mature tree size (for detailed results see **Appendix A**):

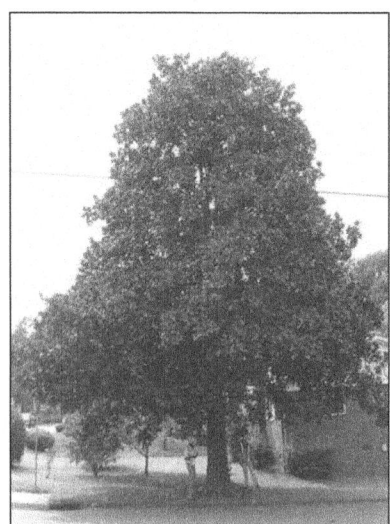

*Figure 14. The Southern magnolia represents medium broadleaf trees in this guide.*

- $7 to $18 for a small tree

- $23 to $35 for a medium tree

- $79 to $92 for a large tree

- $28 to $44 for a conifer

Our findings demonstrate that average annual net benefits from large trees, like the red maple, can be substantially greater than those from small trees like dogwood. Average annual net benefits for the small, medium, and large broadleaf public trees are $7, $24, and $79, respectively. Conifers provide an intermediate level of benefits, on average $28 for a public tree. The largest average annual net benefits, however, stemmed from yard trees opposite the west-facing wall of a house: $18, $35, $92, and $44, for small, medium, and large broadleaf trees and the conifer, respectively.

The large yard tree opposite a west wall produces a net annual benefit of $195 at year 40. In the same location, 40 years after planting, the dogwood, magnolia, and loblolly pine produce annual net benefits of $43, $98, and $107.

Forty years after planting at a typical public site, the small, medium, and large broadleaf trees and the conifer provide annual net benefits of $22, $72, $174, and $107, respectively.

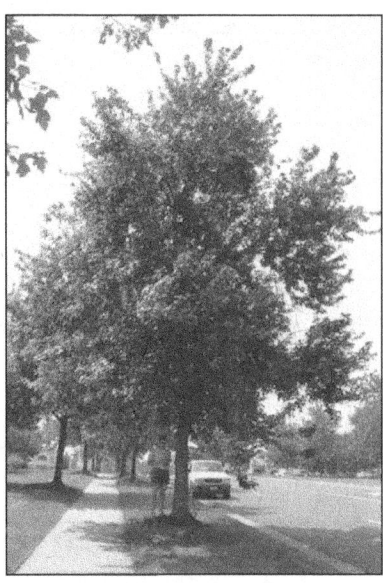

*Figure 15. The red maple represents large broadleaf trees in this guide.*

Net benefits for a yard tree opposite a west house wall and a public tree also increase with size when summed over the entire 40-year period:

*Net benefits summed for 40 years*

- $720 (yard) and $280 (public) for a small tree

- $1,400 (yard) and $960 (public) for a medium tree

- $3,680 (yard) and $3,160 (public) for a large tree

- $1,760 (yard) and $1,120 (public) for a conifer

Twenty years after planting average annual benefits for all trees exceed costs of tree planting and management (**Tables 1** and **2**). For a large red maple in a yard 20 years after planting, the total value of environmental benefits alone ($58) is eight times the total annual cost ($7). Environmental benefits total $29, $31, and $36 for the dogwood, magnolia, and loblolly pine, while tree care costs are similarly lower, $6, $5, and $7, respectively. Adding the value of aesthetics and other benefits to the environmental benefits results in substantial net benefits. Note that the costs for the magnolia and dogwood are similar at 20 years because, at this age, the trees are of similar size.

Net benefits are less for public trees (**Table 2**) than yard trees for two main reasons. First, public tree care costs are greater because they generally receive more intensive care than private trees. Second, energy benefits are lower for public trees than for yard trees because public trees are assumed to provide general climate effects, but not to shade buildings directly.

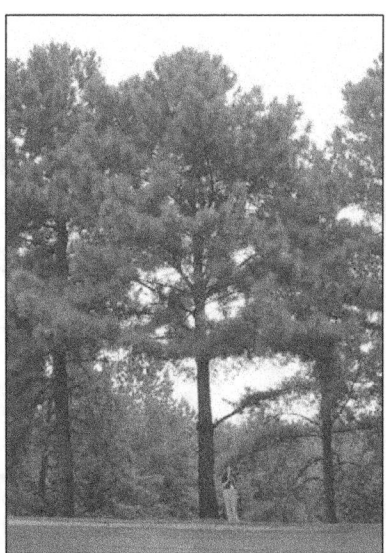

*Figure 16. The loblolly pine represents coniferous trees in this guide.*

*Table 1. Estimated annual benefits and costs for a yard tree opposite a west-facing wall 20 years after planting*

| Benefit category | Flowering dogwood Small tree 28 ft tall 26 ft spread Leaf surface area=653 ft² | | | Southern magnolia Medium tree 32 ft tall 24 ft spread Leaf surface area=1,031 ft² | | | Red maple Large tree 47 ft tall 32 ft spread Leaf surface area=3,332 ft² | | | Loblolly pine Conifer tree 53 ft tall 27 ft spread Leaf surface area=1,318 ft² | | |
|---|---|---|---|---|---|---|---|---|---|---|---|---|
| | RUs | | Total $ | RUs | | Total $ | RUs | | Total $ | RUs | | Total $ |
| Electricity savings ($0 0759/kWh) | 129 | kWh | $9 76 | 143 | kWh | $10 85 | 224 | kWh | $16 99 | 195 4 | kWh | $14 83 |
| Natural gas savings ($0 0105/kBtu) | 236 | kBtu | $2 46 | 121 | kBtu | $1 26 | 363 | kBtu | $3 80 | 192 4 | kBtu | $2 01 |
| Carbon dioxide ($0 0075/lb) | 236 | lb | $1 77 | 167 | lb | $1 25 | 371 | lb | $2 78 | 286 3 | lb | $2 15 |
| Ozone ($6 55/lb) | 0 13 | lb | $0 83 | 0 24 | lb | $1 55 | 0 16 | lb | $1 04 | 0 28 | lb | $1 86 |
| NO$_2$ ($6 55/lb) | 0 22 | lb | $1 47 | 0 25 | lb | $1 65 | 0 38 | lb | $2 46 | 0 35 | lb | $2 27 |
| SO$_2$ ($1 91/lb) | 0 44 | lb | $0 84 | 0 49 | lb | $0 94 | 0 77 | lb | $1 47 | 0 70 | lb | $1 33 |
| PM$_{10}$ ($2 31/lb) | 0 16 | lb | $0 38 | 0 30 | lb | $0 70 | 0 23 | lb | $0 53 | 0 29 | lb | $0 66 |
| VOCs ($6 23/lb) | 0 04 | lb | $0 23 | 0 04 | lb | $0 23 | 0 06 | lb | $0 40 | 0 05 | lb | $0 34 |
| BVOCs ($6 23/lb) | 0 00 | lb | $0 00 | -0 67 | lb | -$4 15 | -0 23 | lb | -$1 43 | -1 52 | lb | -$9 49 |
| Rainfall interception ($0 0099/gal) | 1,098 | gal | $10 87 | 1,656 | gal | $16 39 | 3,067 | gal | $30 36 | 2,074 | gal | $20 53 |
| **Environmental subtotal** | | | **$28.61** | | | **$30.68** | | | **$58.41** | | | **$36.49** |
| Other benefits | | | $6 98 | | | $13 51 | | | $38 75 | | | $20 17 |
| **Total benefits** | | | **$35.59** | | | **$44.18** | | | **$97.15** | | | **$56.66** |
| **Total costs (see Table 3)** | | | **$5.91** | | | **$5.38** | | | **$7.41** | | | **$3.42** |
| **Net benefits** | | | **$29.68** | | | **$38.81** | | | **$89.74** | | | **$53.24** |

**RU** Resource unit

*Table 2. Estimated annual benefits and costs for a public tree (street/park) 20 years after planting*

| Benefit category | Flowering dogwood Small tree 28 ft tall 26 ft spread Leaf surface area=653 ft² | | | Southern magnolia Medium tree 32 ft tall 24 ft spread Leaf surface area=1,031 ft² | | | Red maple Large tree 47 ft tall 32 ft spread Leaf surface area=3,332 ft² | | | Loblolly pine Conifer tree 53 ft tall 27 ft spread Leaf surface area=1,318 ft² | | |
|---|---|---|---|---|---|---|---|---|---|---|---|---|
| | RUs | | Total $ | RUs | | Total $ | RUs | | Total $ | RUs | | Total $ |
| Electricity savings ($0 0759/kWh) | 46 | kWh | $3 47 | 40 | kWh | $3 01 | 69 | kWh | $5 25 | 50 0 | kWh | $3 80 |
| Natural gas savings ($0 0105/kBtu) | 297 | kBtu | $3 10 | 269 | kBtu | $2 81 | 421 | kBtu | $4 40 | 317 | kBtu | $3 32 |
| Carbon dioxide ($0 0075/lb) | 173 | lb | $1 30 | 97 | lb | $0 73 | 247 | lb | $1 85 | 178 1 | lb | $1 34 |
| Ozone ($6 55/lb) | 0 13 | lb | $0 83 | 0 24 | lb | $1 55 | 0 16 | lb | $1 04 | 0 28 | lb | $1 86 |
| NO$_2$ ($6 55/lb) | 0 22 | lb | $1 47 | 0 25 | lb | $1 65 | 0 38 | lb | $2 46 | 0 35 | lb | $2 27 |
| SO$_2$ ($1 91/lb) | 0 44 | lb | $0 84 | 0 49 | lb | $0 94 | 0 77 | lb | $1 47 | 0 70 | lb | $1 33 |
| PM$_{10}$ ($2 31/lb) | 0 16 | lb | $0 38 | 0 30 | lb | $0 70 | 0 23 | lb | $0 53 | 0 29 | lb | $0 66 |
| VOCs ($6 23/lb) | 0 04 | lb | $0 23 | 0 04 | lb | $0 23 | 0 06 | lb | $0 40 | 0 05 | lb | $0 34 |
| BVOCs ($6 23/lb) | 0 00 | lb | $0 00 | -0 67 | lb | -$4 15 | -0 23 | lb | -$1 43 | -1 52 | lb | -$9 49 |
| Rainfall interception ($0 0099/gal) | 1,098 | gal | $10 87 | 1,656 | gal | $16 39 | 3,067 | gal | $30 36 | 2,074 | gal | $20 53 |
| **Environmental subtotal** | | | **$22.49** | | | **$23 86** | | | **$46.34** | | | **$25.95** |
| Other benefits | | | $7 79 | | | $15 09 | | | $43 28 | | | $22 53 |
| **Total benefits** | | | **$30.28** | | | **$38 95** | | | **$89.62** | | | **$48.48** |
| **Total costs (See Table 3)** | | | **$20.65** | | | **$18 54** | | | **$22.33** | | | **$19.98** |
| **Net benefits** | | | **$9.64** | | | **$20.41** | | | **$67.29** | | | **$28.50** |

**RU** Resource unit

## Average Annual Costs

Averaged over 40 years, the annual costs for yard and public trees, respectively, are as follows:

- $18 and $ 24 for a small tree

- $18 and $24 for a medium tree

- $19 and $27 for a large tree

- $16 and $25 for a conifer

As noted above, the costs for the small and medium trees are similar because for the first part of their lives, they grow at similar rates and reach similar sizes.

Over the 40-year period, tree pruning is the single greatest cost for public trees, averaging approximately $6 to $8 per tree per year (see **Appendix A**). Annualized expenditures for tree planting are an important cost, especially for trees planted in private yards ($12.50 per tree per year). Based on our survey, we assume in this study that a yard tree with a 3-in **diameter at breast height** (DBH) is planted at a cost of $500. The cost for planting a 2.5-in public tree is $220 or $5.50 per tree per year. The second greatest annual cost for broadleaf yard trees is for pruning ($2 to $3 per tree per year).

*Greatest costs for pruning and planting*

**Table 3** shows annual management costs 20 years after planting for yard trees to the west of a house and for public trees. Annual costs for yard trees range from $3 to $7, while public tree care costs are $19

*Public trees are more expensive to maintain than yard trees*

*Table 3. Estimated annual costs 20 years after planting for a yard tree opposite a west-facing wall and a public tree*

| Costs ($/year/tree) | Flowering dogwood Small tree 28 ft tall 26 ft spread Leaf surface area=653 ft² | | Southern magnolia Medium tree 32 ft tall 24 ft spread Leaf surface area=1,031 ft² | | Red maple Large tree 47 ft tall 32 ft spread Leaf surface area=3,332 ft² | | Loblolly pine Conifer tree 53 ft tall 27 ft spread Leaf surface area=1,318 ft² | |
|---|---|---|---|---|---|---|---|---|
| | Yard: west | Public tree | Yard: west | Public tree | Yard: west | Public tree | Yard: west | Public tree |
| Pruning | 2 69 | 7 88 | 2 69 | 7 88 | 4 21 | 9 60 | 0 05 | 6 60 |
| Remove & dispose | 1 38 | 4 85 | 1 16 | 4 05 | 1 38 | 4 83 | 1 45 | 5 08 |
| Pest & disease | 1 09 | 0 00 | 0 91 | 0 00 | 1 09 | 0 00 | 1 15 | 0 01 |
| Infrastructure | 0 60 | 4 04 | 0 50 | 3 38 | 0 60 | 4 03 | 0 63 | 4 24 |
| Irrigation | 0 00 | 0 00 | 0 00 | 0 00 | 0 00 | 0 00 | 0 00 | 0 00 |
| Clean-up | 0 07 | 0 45 | 0 06 | 0 38 | 0 07 | 0 45 | 0 07 | 0 47 |
| Liability & legal | 0 07 | 0 44 | 0 06 | 0 37 | 0 07 | 0 44 | 0 07 | 0 46 |
| Admin & other | 0 00 | 2 99 | 0 00 | 2 49 | 0 00 | 2 98 | 0 00 | 3 13 |
| **Total costs** | **5.91** | **20.65** | **5 38** | **18.54** | **7.41** | **22.33** | **3.42** | **19.98** |
| Total benefits | 35 59 | 30 28 | 44 18 | 38 95 | 97 15 | 89 62 | 56 66 | 48 48 |
| **Total net benefits** | **29.68** | **9.64** | **38 81** | **20.41** | **89.74** | **67.29** | **53.24** | **28.50** |

Prices for removal and disposal are included to account for expected mortality of citywide planting

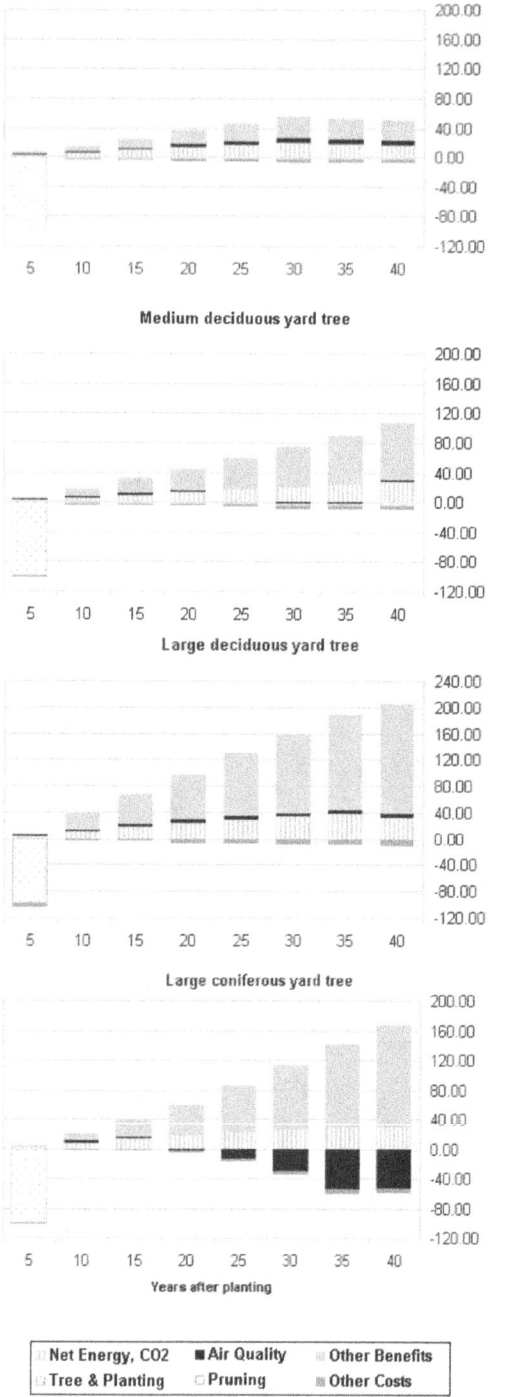

**Small deciduous yard tree**

**Medium deciduous yard tree**

**Large deciduous yard tree**

**Large coniferous yard tree**

Years after planting

Annual benefits and costs ($/tree)

| Net Energy, CO2 | ■ Air Quality | Other Benefits |
| Tree & Planting | Pruning | Other Costs |

*Figure 17. Estimated annual benefits and costs for a large (red maple), medium (Southern magnolia), and small (dogwood) broadleaf tree and a conifer (loblolly pine) located west of a residence. Costs are greatest during the initial establishment period while benefits increase with tree size.*

to $22. In general, public trees are more expensive to maintain than yard trees because of their prominence and because of the greater need for public safety.

## Average Annual Benefits

Average annual benefits over 40 years, including stormwater reduction, aesthetic value, air quality improvement and $CO_2$ sequestration increase with mature tree size (**Figures 17** and **18**, for detailed results see **Appendix A**):

- $31 to $36 for a small tree

- $41 to $53 for a medium tree

- $103 to $112 for a large tree

- $47 to $60 for a conifer

### Stormwater Runoff Reduction

Benefits associated with rainfall interception, reducing stormwater runoff, are substantial for all tree types. The red maple intercepts 4,778 gal/year (18.0 m³/year) on average over a 40-year period with an implied value of $47. The dogwood, magnolia, and loblolly pine intercept 1,265 gal/year (5.7 m³/year), 2,566 gal/year (11.7 m³/year), and 3,888 gal/year (17.7 m³/year) on average, with values of $13, $25, and $38, respectively.

The Piedmont includes some of the fastest growing cities in the United States—areas with increasing amounts of impervious surface. The role that trees can play here in reducing stormwater runoff is substantial.

### Aesthetic and Other Benefits

Benefits associated with property value account for the second largest portion of total benefits. As trees grow and become more visible, they can increase a property's sales price. Average annual values associated with these aesthetic and other benefits for yard trees are $7, $12, $37, and $21 for the small, medium, and large broadleaf trees and for the conifer, respectively. The values for public trees are $7, $13, $41, and $23, respectively. The values for yard trees are slightly less than for public trees because off-street trees contribute less to a property's curb appeal than more prominent street trees. Because our estimates are based on median home sale prices, the effects of trees on property values and aesthetics will vary depending on local economies.

*Energy Savings*

Trees provide significant energy benefits, which tend to increase with tree size. For example, average annual net energy benefits are $11 for the small dogwood opposite a west-facing wall, and $21 for the larger red maple. Average annual net energy benefits for public trees are less than for yard trees because public trees are assumed to provide general climate effects, but not to shade buildings directly. Benefits range from $6 for the dogwood to $11 for the red maple. For species of all sizes, energy savings increase as trees mature and their leaf surface areas increase (**Figures 17 and 18**).

As expected in a region with hot, humid summers and relatively mild winters, cooling savings account for most of the total energy benefit. Average annual cooling savings for the dogwood and red maple range from $3 to $9 and $7 to $16, respectively. Average annual heating savings for the same species range from $1 to $3 and $2 to $4. A magnolia or a loblolly pine planted on the southern side of a house will have a negative effect ($−4 each) on heating because it blocks the warm southern rays of the winter sun (see also **Figure 4**).

Average annual net energy benefits for residential trees are greatest for a tree located west of a building because the effect of shade on cooling costs is maximized. A yard tree located south of a building produces the least net energy benefit because it has the least benefit during summer, and the greatest

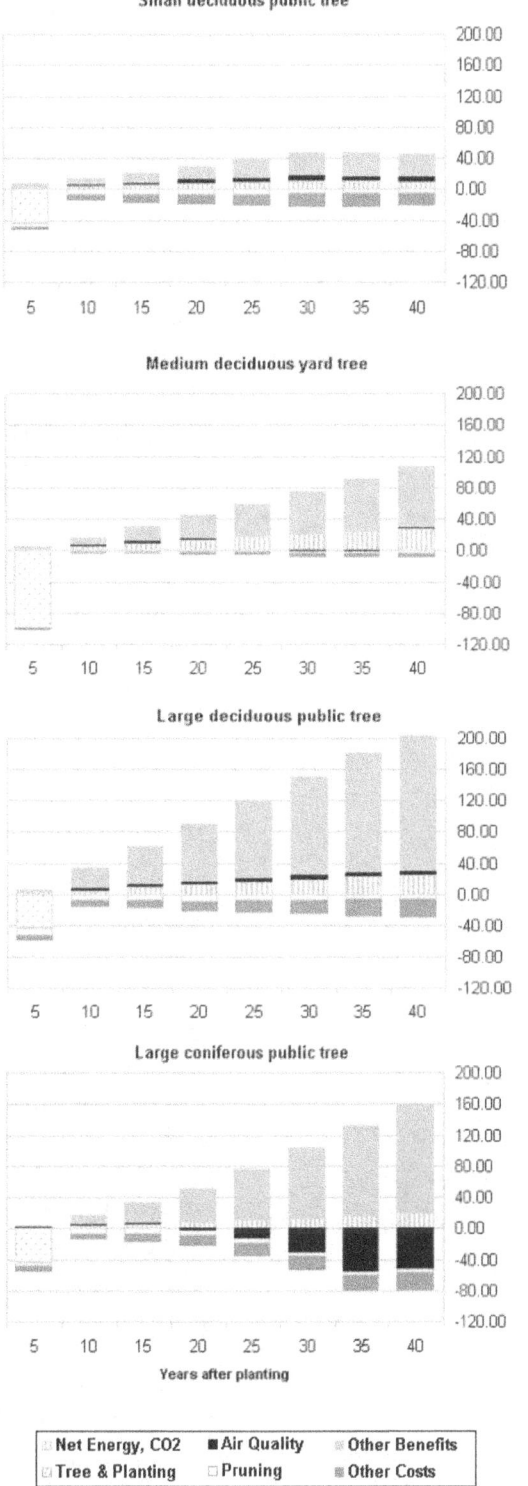

Figure 18. Estimated annual benefits and costs for a large (red maple), medium (Southern magnolia), and small (dogwood) broadleaf tree and a conifer (loblolly pine) public tree.

adverse effect on heating costs from shade in winter. Trees located east of a building provide intermediate net benefits. Net energy benefits also reflect species-related traits such as size, form, branch pattern and density, and time in leaf.

### Carbon Dioxide Reduction

*All tree types reduce CO$_2$*

Net atmospheric CO$_2$ reductions accrue for all tree types. Average annual net reductions range from a high of 441 lbs (200 kg) ($3.31) for a large tree on the west side of a house to a low of 76 lbs (34 kg) ($0.57) for the medium tree on the southern side of the house. Deciduous trees opposite west-facing house walls produced the greatest CO$_2$ reduction due to avoided power plant emissions associated with energy savings. The values for the Southern magnolia are lowest for CO$_2$ reduction because of the negative impacts of the dense, low-growing evergreen foliage on winter heating needs.

Forty years after planting, average annual avoided emissions and sequestered and released CO$_2$ for a yard tree opposite a west wall are 310 lbs (141 kg), 395 lbs (179 kg), 815 lbs (370 kg) and 582 lbs (264 kg), respectively, for the small, medium, and large broadleaf trees and the conifer. Releases of CO$_2$ associated with tree care activities account for less than 1% of net CO$_2$ sequestration.

### Air Quality Improvement

*Annual air quality benefits*

Air-quality benefits are defined as the sum of pollutant uptake by trees and avoided power plant emissions due to energy savings minus biogenic volatile organic compounds (BVOCs) released by trees. Average annual air quality benefits range from $19 to $4 per tree. The negative values for loblolly pines ($19 per tree) result from this species' high emissions of BVOCs (4.4 lbs per year), which contribute to ozone formation. These high levels exceed the air quality benefits related to other pollutants.

The total average annual air quality benefit is a relatively low $0.61 for the Southern magnolia—also an emitter of BVOCs. Larger benefits are estimated for the small tree and the large tree ($3.75 and $3.97 per year).

Different species have different air quality strengths. The dogwood, for instance, is particularly good at reducing pollutants related to ozone formation. Total O$_3$ and NO$_2$ uptake and avoidance for dogwood averaged 0.36 lbs per year, valued at $2.35. The evergreen loblolly pine is especially effective at reducing SO$_2$ and PM$_{10}$, removing almost a pound (0.77 lb, 0.35 kg) of SO$_2$ and half a pound (0.47 lb, 0.21 kg) of PM$_{10}$ each year, valued at $1.48 and $1.08, respectively.

# Chapter 4. Estimating Benefits and Costs for Tree Planting Projects in Your Community

This chapter shows two ways that benefit–cost information presented in this guide can be used. The first hypothetical example demonstrates how to adjust values from the guide for local conditions when the goal is to estimate benefits and costs for a proposed tree planting project. The second example explains how to compare net benefits derived from planting different types of trees. The last section discusses actions communities can take to increase the cost-effectiveness of their tree programs.

## *Applying Benefit–Cost Data*

### *Wild Ramp City Example*

The city of Wild Ramp is located in the Piedmont region and has a population of 24,000. Most of its street trees were planted in the 1930s, with silver maple (**Acer saccharinum**) and willow oak (**Quercus phellos**) as the dominant species. Currently, the tree canopy cover is sparse because most of the trees have died and not been replaced. Many of the remaining street trees are in declining health. The city hired an urban forester two years ago and an active citizens' group, the Green Team, has formed (**Figure 19**).

Initial discussions among the Green Team, local utilities, the urban forester, and other partners led to a proposed urban forestry program. The program intends to plant 1,000 trees in Wild Ramp over a five-year period. Trained volunteers will plant ¾- to 1-inch trees in the following proportions: 70% large-maturing trees, 15% medium-maturing trees and 5% small-maturing trees and 10% conifers. The total cost for planting will be $160 per tree. One hundred trees will be planted in parks, and the remaining 900 trees will be planted along Main Street and other downtown streets.

The Wild Ramp City Council has agreed to maintain the current funding level for management of existing trees. Also, they will advocate formation of a municipal tree district to

*Figure 19. The Green Team is gung-ho to re-green their community by planting 1,000 trees in five years.*

raise funds for the proposed tree-planting project. A municipal tree district is similar in concept to a landscape assessment district, which receives revenues based on formulas that account for the services different customers receive. For example, the proximity of customers to greenspace in a landscape assessment district may determine how much they pay for upkeep. A municipal tree district might receive funding from air quality districts, stormwater management agencies, electric utilities, businesses, and residents in proportion to the value of future benefits these groups will receive from trees in terms of air quality, hydrology, energy, $CO_2$, and property value. Such a district would require voter approval of a special assessment that charges recipients for tree planting and maintenance costs in proportion to the tangible benefits they receive from the new trees. The Council needs to know the amount of funding required for tree planting and maintenance, as well as how the benefits will be distributed over the 40-year life of the project.

*The first step: Determine tree planting numbers and local prices*

As a first step, the Wild Ramp city forester and Green Team decided to use the tables in **Appendix A** to quantify total cumulative benefits and costs over 40 years for the proposed planting of 1,000 public trees—700 large, 150 medium, and 50 small broadleaf trees and 100 conifers.

Before setting up a spreadsheet to calculate benefits and costs, the team considered which aspects of Wild Ramp's urban and community forestry project differ from the regional values used in this guide (the methods for calculating the values in **Appendix A** are described in **Appendix B**):

1.  The prices of electricity and natural gas in Wild Ramp are $0.11/**kWh** and $0.0097/**kBtu**, not $0.0759/kWh and $0.0105/kBtu as assumed in the Guide. It is assumed that the buildings that will be shaded by the new street trees have air conditioning and natural-gas heating.

2.  The Green Team projected future annual costs for monitoring tree health and implementing their stewardship program. Administration costs are estimated to average $2,500 annually for the life of the trees or $2.50 per tree each year. This guide assumed an average annual administration cost of $3.00 per tree for large public trees. Thus, an adjustment is necessary.

3.  Planting will cost $160 per tree. The Guide assumes planting costs of $220 per tree. The costs will be slightly lower for Wild Ramp because the labor will be provided by trained volunteers.

To calculate the dollar value of total benefits and costs for the 40-year period, the forester created a spreadsheet table (**Table 4**). Each benefit and cost category is listed in the first column. Prices, some adjusted for Wild Ramp and some not, are entered into the second column. The third column contains the **resource units** (RU) per tree per year associated with the benefit or the cost per tree per year, which can be found in **Appendix A**. For aesthetic and other benefits, the dollar values for public trees are placed in the resource unit columns. The fourth column lists the 40-year total values, obtained by multiplying the RU values by tree numbers, prices, and 40 years.

To adjust for higher electricity prices, the forester multiplied electricity saved for a large public tree in the RU column (89 kWh) by the Wild Ramp price for electricity ($0.11/kWh). This value ($9.79 per tree per year) was then multiplied by the number of trees planted and 40 years ($9.79 × 700 trees × 40 years = $273,426) to obtain cumulative air-conditioning energy savings for the large public trees (**Table 4**). The process was carried out for all benefits and all tree types.

*The second step: Adjust for local prices of benefits*

Table 4. *Spreadsheet calculations for the Wild Ramp planting project (1,000 trees), benefits and costs over 40 years*

| Benefits | Price ($) | 700 large trees RU/tree/yr | 700 large trees Total $ | 150 medium trees RU/tree/yr | 150 medium trees Total $ | 50 small trees RU/tree/yr | 50 small trees Total $ | 100 conifers RU/tree/yr | 100 conifers Total $ | 1000 total trees Total $ | 1000 total trees $/tree/yr | % benefits |
|---|---|---|---|---|---|---|---|---|---|---|---|---|
| Electricity (kWh) | 0 11 | 89 | 273,426 | 53 | 34,673 | 44 | 9,748 | 66 | 28,844 | 346,691 | 8 67 | 9 6 |
| Natural gas (kBtu) | 0 0097 | 415 | 112,692 | 298 | 17,333 | 278 | 5,389 | 337 | 13,078 | 148,492 | 3 71 | 4 1 |
| Net $CO_2$ (lb) | 0 0075 | 340 | 71,366 | 318 | 14,310 | 168 | 2,514 | 227 | 6,825 | 95,016 | 2 38 | 2 6 |
| Ozone (lb) | 6 55 | 0 21 | 38,841 | 0 35 | 13,618 | 0 14 | 1,839 | 0 42 | 10,958 | 65,256 | 1 63 | 1 8 |
| $NO_2$ (lb) | 6 55 | 0 41 | 75,850 | 0 33 | 12,793 | 0 22 | 2,856 | 0 42 | 10,900 | 102,398 | 2 56 | 2 8 |
| $SO_2$ (lb) | 1 91 | 0 82 | 44,069 | 0 60 | 6,923 | 0 42 | 1,600 | 0 77 | 5,914 | 58,505 | 1 46 | 1 6 |
| $PM_{10}$ (lb) | 2 31 | 0 31 | 20,012 | 0 56 | 7,735 | 0 17 | 773 | 0 47 | 4,314 | 32,834 | 0 82 | 0 9 |
| VOCs (lb) | 6 23 | 0 07 | 11,950 | 0 05 | 1,693 | 0 03 | 430 | 0 06 | 1,464 | 15,537 | 0 39 | 0 4 |
| BVOCs (lb) | 6 23 | -0 46 | -79,722 | -1 05 | -39,127 | 0 00 | 0 | -4 36 | -108,702 | -227,550 | -5 69 | -6 3 |
| Hydrology (gal) | 0 0099 | 4,778 | 1,324,463 | 2,566 | 152,419 | 1,265 | 25,038 | 3,888 | 153,967 | 1,655,887 | 41 40 | 45 6 |
| Aesthetics & other | | 41 02 | 1,148,669 | 13 44 | 80,650 | 7 29 | 14,582 | 23 08 | 92,338 | 1,336,238 | 33 41 | 36 8 |
| Total benefits | | | 3,041,617 | | 303,019 | | 64,770 | | 219,900 | 3,629,305 | 90 73 | 100 0 |

| Costs | | $/tree/yr | Total $ | $/tree/yr | Total $ | $/tree/yr | Total $ | $/tree/yr | Total $ | Total $ | $/tree/yr | % costs |
|---|---|---|---|---|---|---|---|---|---|---|---|---|
| Tree & planting | | 4 00 | 112,000 | 4 00 | 24,000 | 4 00 | 8,000 | 4 00 | 16,000 | 160,000 | 4 00 | 16 5 |
| Pruning | | 8 34 | 233,397 | 7 65 | 45,879 | 7 11 | 14,225 | 6 19 | 24,761 | 318,263 | 7 96 | 32 8 |
| Remove & dispose | | 5 32 | 149,000 | 4 29 | 25,739 | 4 70 | 9,395 | 5 26 | 21,022 | 205,156 | 5 13 | 21 2 |
| Infrastructure repair | | 3 95 | 110,473 | 3 24 | 19,462 | 3 54 | 7,088 | 3 93 | 15,729 | 152,752 | 3 82 | 15 8 |
| Clean-up | | 0 44 | 12,275 | 0 36 | 2,162 | 0 39 | 788 | 0 44 | 1,748 | 16,972 | 0 42 | 1 8 |
| Liability & legal | | 0 43 | 12,067 | 0 35 | 2,126 | 0 39 | 774 | 0 43 | 1,718 | 16,685 | 0 42 | 1 7 |
| Admin & other | | 2 50 | 70,000 | 2 50 | 15,000 | 2 50 | 5,000 | 2 50 | 10,000 | 100,000 | 2 50 | 10 3 |
| Total costs | | | 699,212 | | 134,369 | | 45,270 | | 90,977 | 969,828 | 24 25 | 100 0 |
| Net benefit | | | 2,342,405 | | 168,650 | | 19,500 | | 128,922 | 2,659,477 | 66 49 | |
| Benefit/cost ratio | | | 4 35 | | 2 26 | | 1 43 | | 2 42 | | 3 74 | |

RU Resource unit

41

*The third step: Adjust for local costs*

To adjust cost figures, the city forester changed the planting cost from $220 assumed in the Guide to $160 (**Table 4**). This planting cost was annualized by dividing the cost per tree by 40 years ($160/40 = $4.00 per tree per year). Total planting costs were calculated by multiplying this value by 700 large trees and 40 years ($112,000).

The administration, inspection, and outreach costs are expected to average $2.50 per tree per year, or a total of $100 per tree for the project's life. Consequently, the total administration cost for large trees is $2.50 × 700 large trees × 40 years ($70,000). The same procedure was followed to calculate costs for the medium and small broadleaf trees and conifers.

*The fourth step: Calculate net benefits and benefit–cost ratios for public trees*

Subtracting total costs from total benefits yields net benefits:

- Small broadleaf trees: $19,500 or $9.75 per tree per year

- Medium broadleaf trees: $168,650 or $28.11 per tree per year

- Large broadleaf trees: $2,342,405 over 40 years or $83.66 per tree per year

- Conifers: $128,922 or $32.23 per tree per year

Annual benefits over 40 years total $3.6 million ($91 per tree per year), and annual costs total a little less than $1 million ($24 per tree per year). The total net annual benefits for all 1,000 trees over the 40-year period are $2.7 million, or $66 per tree. To calculate the average annual net benefit per tree, the forester divided the total net benefit by the number of trees planted (1,000) and 40 years ($2,659,477 / 1,000 trees / 40 years = $66.49). Dividing total benefits by total costs yielded benefit–cost ratios (BCRs) that ranged from 1.43 for small trees, to 2.26, 4.35 and 2.42 for medium and large broadleaf trees and conifers. The BCR for the entire planting is 3.74, indicating that $3.74 will be returned for every $1 invested.

It is important to remember that this analysis assumes 45% of the planted trees die and does not account for the time value of money from a municipal capital investment perspective. Use the municipal discount rate to compare this investment in tree planting and management with alternative municipal investments.

*The final step: Determine how benefits are distributed and link these to sources of revenue*

The city forester and Green Team now know that the project will cost about $1 million, and the average annual cost will be $24,250 ($970,000 / 40 years); however, more funds will be needed initially for planting and irrigation. The fifth and last step is to identify the distribution of functional benefits that the trees will provide. The last column in Table 4 shows the distribution of positive benefits as a percentage of the total:

- Energy savings = 14% (cooling = 10%, heating = 4%)

- Carbon dioxide reduction = 3%

- Stormwater-runoff reduction = 45%

- Aesthetics/property value increase = 37%

- Air quality = 1%

With this information the planning team can determine how to distribute the costs for tree planting and maintenance based on who benefits from the services the trees will provide. For example, assuming the goal is to generate enough annual revenue to cover the total costs of managing the trees ($1 million), fees could be distributed in the following manner:

*Distributing costs of tree management to multiple parties*

- $140,000 from electric and natural gas utilities for energy savings (14%)

- $30,000 from local industry for atmospheric carbon dioxide reductions (3%)

- $450,000 from the stormwater-management district for water quality improvement associated with reduced runoff (45%)

- $370,000 from property owners for increased property values (37%)

- $10,000 from air quality management district for net reduction in air pollutants (1%)

Whether project funds are sought from partners, the general fund, or other sources, this information can assist managers in developing policy, setting priorities, and making decisions. The Center for Urban Forest Research has developed a computer program called STRATUM that simplifies these calculations for analysis of existing street tree populations (Maco and McPherson 2003; http://cufr.ucdavis.edu).

### City of Bassville Example

As a municipal cost-cutting measure, the city of Bassville plans to stop planting street trees in areas of new development. Instead, developers will be required to plant front yard trees, thereby reducing costs to the city. The community forester and concerned citizens believe that, although this policy will result in lower planting costs, developers may plant smaller trees than the city would have. Currently, Bassville's policy is to plant as large a tree as possible based on each site's available growing space (**Figure 20**). Planting smaller trees could result in benefits "forgone" that will exceed cost savings. To evaluate this possible outcome the community forester and concerned citizens decided to compare costs and benefits of planting large, medium, and small trees for a hypothetical street-tree planting project in Bassville.

*The first step: Determine tree numbers and local prices*

As a first step, the city forester and concerned citizens decided to quantify the total cumulative benefits and costs over 40 years for a typical street tree planting of 1,500 trees in Bassville. For comparison purposes, the planting includes 500 large trees, 500 medium trees, and 500 small trees. Data in **Appendix A** are used for the calculations; however, three aspects of Bassville's urban and community forestry program are different than assumed in this tree guide:

1. The price of electricity is $0.09/kWh, not $0.0759/kWh.

2. The trees will be irrigated for the first five years at a cost of approximately $0.50 per tree annually.

*Figure 20. Bassville's policy to plant as large a tree as the site will handle has provided ample benefits in the past. Here, large-stature trees have been planted.*

44

3. Planting costs are $250 per tree for city trees instead of the $220 per tree.

To calculate the dollar value of total benefits and costs for the 40-year period, the last column in **Appendix A** (40-year average) is multiplied by 40 years. Since this value is for one tree it must be multiplied by the total number of trees planted in the respective large, medium, or small tree size classes. To adjust for higher electricity prices we multiply electricity saved for each tree type in the resource unit column by the number of trees and 40 years (large tree: 89 kWh × 500 trees × 40 years = 1,780,000 kWh). This value is multiplied by the price of electricity in Bassville ($0.09/kWh × 1,780,000 kWh = $160,200) to obtain cumulative air-conditioning energy savings for the project (**Table 5**).

*The second step: Calculate benefits and costs over 40 years*

All the benefits are summed for each size tree for a 40-year period. The 500 large trees provide $2.1 million in total benefits. The medium and small trees provide $961,200 and $629,600, respectively.

To adjust cost figures, we add a value for irrigation by multiplying the annual cost by the number of trees by the number of years irrigation

Table 5. *Spreadsheet calculations for the Bassville planting project (1,500 trees), benefits and costs over 40 years*

| | 500 Large trees | | 500 Medium trees | | 500 Small trees | | 1,500 Trees total | | Average | |
|---|---|---|---|---|---|---|---|---|---|---|
| Benefits | RUs | Total $ | RUs | Total $ | RUs | Total $ | RUs | Total $ | $/tree | % benefits |
| Electricity (kWh) | 1,780,000 | 160,200 | 1,060,000 | 95,400 | 880,000 | 79,200 | 3,720,000 | 334,800 | 223 | 9 0 |
| Natural gas (kBtu) | 8,300,000 | 80,600 | 5,960,000 | 57,800 | 5,560,000 | 54,000 | 19,820,000 | 192,400 | 128 | 5 2 |
| Net $CO_2$ (lb) | 6,800,000 | 51,000 | 2,560,000 | 19,200 | 3,360,000 | 25,200 | 12,720,000 | 95,400 | 64 | 2 6 |
| Ozone (lb) | 4,230 | 27,800 | 6,930 | 45,400 | 2,810 | 18,400 | 13,970 | 91,600 | 61 | 4 5 |
| $NO_2$ (lb) | 8,270 | 54,200 | 6,510 | 42,600 | 4,360 | 28,600 | 19,140 | 125,400 | 84 | |
| $SO_2$ (lb) | 16,470 | 31,400 | 12,070 | 23,000 | 0 | 16,000 | 28,540 | 70,400 | 47 | |
| $PM_{10}$ (lb) | 6,190 | 14,200 | 11,160 | 25,800 | 3,340 | 7,800 | 20,690 | 47,800 | 32 | 4 5 |
| VOCs (lb) | 1,370 | 8,600 | 910 | 5,600 | 690 | 4,200 | 2,970 | 18,400 | 12 | |
| BVOCs (lb) | -9,140 | -57,000 | -20,940 | -130,400 | 0 | 0 | -30,080 | -187,400 | -125 | |
| Hydrology (gal) | 95,560,000 | 946,000 | 51,320,000 | 508,000 | 25,300,000 | 250,400 | 172,180,000 | 1,704,400 | 1,136 | 45 7 |
| Aesthetics and other benefits | | 820,400 | | 268,800 | | 145,800 | | 1,235,000 | 823 | 33 1 |
| Total benefits | | 2,137,400 | | 961,200 | | 629,600 | | 3,728,200 | 2,485 | 100 0 |

| Costs | Total $ | Total $ | Total $ | Total $ | $/tree | % benefits |
|---|---|---|---|---|---|---|
| Tree & planting | 125,000 | 125,000 | 125,000 | 375,000 | 250 | 24 2 |
| Pruning | 166,800 | 153,000 | 142,200 | 462,000 | 308 | 29 9 |
| Remove & dispose | 106,400 | 85,800 | 94,000 | 286,200 | 191 | 18 5 |
| Infrastructure | 79,000 | 64,800 | 70,800 | 214,600 | 143 | 13 9 |
| Irrigation | 1,250 | 1,250 | 1,250 | 3,750 | 3 | 0 2 |
| Clean-up | 8,800 | 7,200 | 7,800 | 23,800 | 16 | 1 5 |
| Liability & legal | 8,600 | 7,000 | 7,800 | 23,400 | 16 | 1 5 |
| Admin & other | 58,400 | 48,000 | 52,400 | 158,800 | 106 | 10 3 |
| Total costs | 554,250 | 492,050 | 501,250 | 1,547,550 | 1,032 | 100 0 |
| **Net benefits** | **1,583,150** | **469,150** | **128,350** | **2,180,650** | **1,453** | |
| **Benefit / cost ratio** | **3.86** | **1 95** | **1.26** | **2.41** | | |

RU=Resource unit

*The third step: Adjust for local costs*

will be applied ($0.50 × 500 trees × 5 years = $1,250). We multiply 500 large trees by the unit planting cost ($250) to obtain the adjusted cost for planting in Bassville (500 × $250 = $125,000). The average annual 40-year costs taken from **Appendix A** for other items are multiplied by 40 years and the appropriate number of trees to compute total costs. These 40-year cost values are entered into **Table 5**.

*The fourth step: Calculate cost savings and benefits forgone*

Subtracting total costs from total benefits yields net benefits for the large ($1,583,150), medium ($469,150), and small ($128,350) trees. The total net benefits for the 40-year period are $2.18 million (total benefits ☐ total costs), or $1,453 per tree ($2.18 million/1,500 trees) on average (**Table 5**).

The net benefits per public tree planted are as follows:

*Net benefit per tree*

- $257 for a small tree

- $938 for a medium tree

- $3,166 for a large tree

By not investing in street tree planting, the city would save $375,000 in initial planting costs. There is a risk, however, that developers will not plant the largest trees possible. If the developer planted 1,500 small trees, benefits would total $1.9 million (3 x $629,600 for 500 small trees). If 1,500 large trees were planted, benefits would total $6.4 million. Planting all small trees causes the city to forgo benefits valued at $4.5 million. This amount far exceeds the savings of $375,000 obtained by requiring developers to plant new street trees, and suggests that, when turning over the responsibility for tree planting to others, the city should be very careful to develop and enforce a street tree ordinance that requires planting large trees where feasible.

Based on this analysis, the City of Bassville decided to retain the policy of promoting planting of large trees where space permits. They now require tree shade plans that show how developers will achieve 50% shade over streets, sidewalks, and parking lots within 15 years of development.

This analysis assumed 45% of the planted trees died. It did not account for the time value of money from a capital investment perspective, but this could be done using the municipal discount rate.

## *Increasing Program Cost-Effectiveness*

*What if costs are too high?*

What if the program you have designed is promising in terms of stormwater-runoff reduction, energy savings, volunteer participation, and additional benefits, but the costs are too high? This section describes some steps to consider that may increase benefits and reduce costs, thereby increasing cost-effectiveness.

## Increasing Benefits

Improved stewardship to increase the health and survival of recently planted trees is one strategy for increasing cost-effectiveness. An evaluation of the Sacramento Shade program found that tree survival rates had a substantial impact on projected benefits (Hildebrandt et al. 1996). Higher survival rates increase energy savings and reduce tree removal and planting costs.

*Work to increase survival rates*

Conifers and broadleaf evergreens intercept rainfall and particulate matter year-round as well as reduce wind speeds and provide shade, which lowers summer-cooling and winter-heating costs. Locating these types of trees in yards, parks, school grounds, and other open-space areas can increase benefits.

*Target tree plantings with highest return*

You can further increase energy benefits by planting a higher percentage of trees in locations that produce the greatest energy savings, such as opposite west-facing walls and close to buildings with air conditioning. Keep in mind that evergreen trees, as demonstrated in this study by the Southern magnolia and the loblolly pine, should not be planted on the southern side of buildings because their branches and leaves block the warm rays of the winter sun. By customizing tree locations to increase numbers in high-yield sites, energy savings can be boosted.

*Customize planting locations*

## Reducing Program Costs

Cost effectiveness is influenced by program costs as well as benefits:

Cost-effectiveness = Total net benefit / total program cost

Cutting costs is one strategy to increase cost effectiveness. A substantial percentage of total program costs occur during the first five years and are associated with tree planting and establishment (McPherson 1993). Some strategies to reduce these costs include:

*Reduce up-front and establishment costs*

- Plant bare-root or smaller tree stock.

- Use trained volunteers for planting and pruning of young trees (**Figure 21**).

- Provide follow-up care to increase tree survival and reduce replacement costs.

- Select and locate trees to avoid conflicts with infrastructure.

Where growing conditions are likely to be favorable, such as yard or garden settings, it may be cost-effective to use smaller, less expensive stock or bare-root tree. In highly urbanized settings and sites subject to vandalism, however, large stock may survive the initial establishment period better than small stock.

*Use less expensive stock where appropriate*

*Early investment pays off*

Investing in the resources needed to promote tree establishment during the first five years after planting is usually worthwhile, because once trees are established they have a high probability of continued survival. If your program has targeted trees on private property, then encourage residents to attend tree-care workshops. Develop standards of "establishment success" for different types of tree species. Perform periodic inspections to alert residents to tree health problems, and reward those whose trees meet your program's establishment standards. Replace dead trees as soon as possible, and identify ways to improve survivability.

*Figure 21. Trained volunteers can plant and maintain young trees, allowing the community to accomplish more at less cost and providing satisfaction for participants.*

Although organizing and training volunteers requires labor and resources, it is usually less costly than contracting the work. A cadre of trained volunteers can easily maintain trees until they reach a height of about 20 ft (6 m) and limbs are too high to prune from the ground with pole pruners. By the time trees reach this size they are well established. Pruning during this establishment period should result in trees that will require less care in the long term. Training young trees can provide a strong branching structure that requires less frequent thinning and shaping (Costello 2000). Ideally, young trees should be inspected and pruned every other year for the first five years after planting.

*Train volunteers to monitor tree health*

As trees grow larger, pruning costs may increase on a per-tree basis. The frequency of pruning will influence these costs, since it takes longer to prune a tree that has not been pruned in 10 years than one that was pruned a few years ago. Although pruning frequency varies by species and location, a return frequency of about five to eight years is usually sufficient for older trees (Miller 1997).

*Prune early*

Carefully select and locate trees to avoid conflicts with overhead power lines, sidewalks, and underground utilities. Time spent planning the planting will result in long-term savings. Also consider soil type and irrigation, microclimate, and the type of activities occurring around the tree that will influence its growth and management.

*Match tree to site*

When evaluating the bottom line—trees pay us back—do not forget to consider benefits other than the stormwater–runoff reductions, energy savings, atmospheric $CO_2$ reductions, and other tangible benefits. The magnitude of benefits related to employment opportunities, job training, community building, reduced violence, and enhanced human health and well-being can be substantial (**Figure 22**). Moreover, these benefits extend beyond the site where trees are planted, furthering collaborative efforts to build better communities.

*It all adds up—trees pay us back*

*Figure 22. Trees pay us back in tangible and intangible ways.*

*Additional information*

Additional information regarding urban and community forestry program design and implementation can be obtained from the following sources:

Bratkovich, S.M. 2001. **Utilizing municipal trees: ideas from across the country.** NA-TP-06-01. Newtown Square, PA: U.S. Department of Agriculture, Forest Service, Northeastern Area State and Private Forestry.

Miller, R.W. 1997. **Urban forestry: planning and managing urban greenspaces.** 2nd Edition. Upper Saddle River, NJ: Prentice-Hall.

Morgan, N.R. Undated. **An introductory guide to community and urban forestry in Washington, Oregon, and California.** Portland, OR: World Forestry Center.

Morgan, N.R. 1993. **A technical guide to urban and community forestry.** Portland, OR: World Forestry Center.

Pokorny, J.D., coord. author. 2003. **Urban tree risk management: a community guide to program design and implementation.** NA-TP-03-03. Newtown Square, PA: U.S. Department of Agriculture, Forest Service, Northeastern Area State and Private Forestry.

Additional information regarding tree planting and care can be obtained from the following references:

Bedker, P.J.; O'Brien, J.G.; Mielke, M.E. 1995. **How to prune trees.** NA-FR-01-95. Newtown Square, PA: U.S. Department of Agriculture, Forest Service, Northeastern Area State and Private Forestry.

Hargrave, R.; Johnson, G.R.; Zins, M.E. 2002. **Planting trees and shrubs for long-term health.** MI-07681-S. St. Paul, MN: University of Minnesota Extension Service.

Hauer, R.J.; Hruska, M.C.; Dawson, J.O. 1994. **Trees and ice storms: The development of ice storm-resistant urban tree populations.** Special Publication 94-1. Urbana, IL: Department of Forestry, University of Illinois at Urbana-Champaign.

Haugen, L.M. 1998. **How to identify and manage Dutch elm disease.** NA-PR-07-98. Newtown Square, PA: U.S. Department of Agriculture, Forest Service, Northeastern Area State and Private Forestry.

O'Brien, J.G.; Mielke, M.E.; Starkey, D.; Juzwik, J. 2000. **How to identify, prevent, and control oak wilt.** NA-PR-03-00. Newtown Square, PA: U.S. Department of Agriculture, Forest Service, Northeastern Area State and Private Forestry.

# Chapter 5. General Guidelines for Selecting and Placing Trees

In this chapter, general guidelines for selecting and locating trees are presented. Residential trees and trees in public places are considered.

## Guidelines for Energy Savings

### Maximizing Energy Savings from Shading

The right tree in the right place can save energy and reduce tree care costs. In midsummer, the sun shines on the east side of a building in the morning, passes over the roof near midday, and then shines on the west side in the afternoon (**Figure 23**). Electricity use is highest during the afternoon when temperatures are warmest and incoming sunshine is greatest. Therefore, the west side of a home is the most important side to shade (Sand 1994).

*Where should shade trees be planted?*

Depending on building orientation and window placement, sun shining through windows can heat a home quickly during the morning hours. The east side is the second most important side to shade when considering the net impact of tree shade on energy savings (**Figure 23**). Deciduous trees on the east side provide summer shade and more winter solar heat gain than evergreens.

*Figure 23. Locate trees to shade west and east windows (from Sand 1993).*

Trees located to shade south walls can block winter sunshine and increase heating costs because during winter the sun is lower in the sky and shines on the south side of homes (**Figure 24**). The warmth the sun provides is an asset, so do not plant evergreen trees that will block southern exposures and solar collectors. Use **solar-friendly trees** to the south because the bare branches of these deciduous trees allow most sunlight to strike the building (some solar-unfriendly deciduous

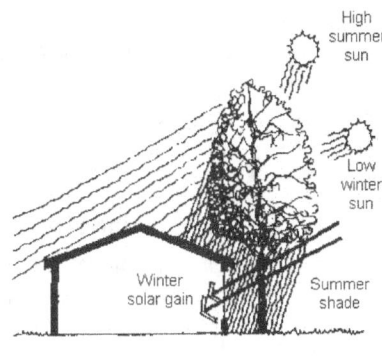

*Figure 24. Select solar-friendly trees for southern exposures and locate them close enough to provide winter solar access and summer shade (from Sand 1991).*

*Figure 25. Trees south of a home before and after pruning. Lower branches are pruned up to increase heat gain from winter sun (from Sand 1993).*

trees can reduce sunlight striking the south side of buildings by 50% even without leaves) (Ames 1987). Examples of solar-friendly trees include most species and **cultivars** of maples (**Acer** spp.), hackberry (**Celtis** spp.), honey locust (**Gleditsia triacanthos**), Kentucky coffee tree (**Gymnocladus dioica**), and pagoda tree (**Sophora japonica**). Some solar-unfriendly trees include most oaks (**Quercus** spp.), sycamore (**Platanus** spp.), most elms (**Ulmus** spp.), basswood (**Tilia americana**), river birch (**Betula nigra**), and horse chestnut (**Aesculus hippocastanum**) (McPherson et al. 1994).

To maximize summer shade and minimize winter shade, locate shade trees about 10–20 ft (3–6 m) south of the home. As trees grow taller, prune lower branches to allow more sun to reach the building if this will not weaken the tree's structure (**Figure 25**).

Although the closer a tree is to a home the more shade it provides, roots of trees that are too close can damage the foundation. Branches that impinge on the building can make it difficult to maintain exterior walls and windows. Keep trees 10 ft (3 m) or further from the home depending on mature crown spread, to avoid these conflicts. Trees within 30–50 ft (9–15 m) of the home most effectively shade windows and walls.

*Patios, driveways and air conditioners need shade*

Paved patios and driveways can become **heat sinks** that warm the home during the day. Shade trees can make them cooler and more comfortable spaces. If a home is equipped with an air conditioner, shading can reduce its energy use, but do not plant vegetation so close that it will obstruct the flow of air around the unit.

*Avoid power, sewer, and water lines*

Plant only small-growing trees under overhead power lines and avoid planting directly above underground water and sewer lines if possible. Contact your local utility company before planting to determine where underground lines are located and which tree species should not be planted below power lines.

## *Planting Windbreaks for Heating Savings*

A tree's size and crown density can make it ideal for blocking wind, thereby reducing the impacts of cold winter weather. Locate rows of trees perpendicular to the prevailing wind (**Figure 26**), usually the north and west side of homes in the Piedmont region.

*Figure 26. Evergreens protect a building from dust and cold by reducing wind speeds (from Sand 1993).*

Design the windbreak row to be longer than the building being sheltered because wind speed increases at the edge of the windbreak. Ideally, the windbreak should be planted upwind about 25–50 ft (7–15 m) from the building and should consist of dense evergreens that will grow to twice the height of the building they shelter (Heisler 1986; Sand 1991). Avoid planting windbreaks that will block sunlight to south and east walls (**Figure 27**). Trees should be spaced close enough to form a dense screen, but not so close that they will block sunlight to each other, causing lower branches to self-prune. Most conifers can be spaced about 6 ft (2 m) on center. If there is room for two or more rows, then space rows 10–12 ft (3–4 m) apart.

Evergreens are preferred over deciduous trees for windbreaks because they provide better wind protection. The ideal windbreak tree is fast growing, visually dense, has strong branch attachments, and has stiff branches that do not self-prune. Large windbreak trees for communities in the Piedmont include white fir (**Abies concolor**), Colorado spruce (**Picea pungens**), spruce pine (**Pinus glabra**), Virginia pine (**Pinus virginiana**) and Southern magnolia (**Magnolia grandiflora**). Good windbreak species for smaller sites include eastern red cedar (**Juniperus virginiana**) and American holly (**Ilex opaca**).

In settings where vegetation is not a fire hazard, evergreens

*Figure 27. Mid-winter shadows from a well-located windbreak and shade trees do not block solar radiation on the south-facing wall (from Sand 1993).*

planted close to the home create airspaces that reduce air infiltration and heat loss. Allow shrubs to form thick hedges, especially along north, west, and east walls.

## Selecting Trees to Maximize Benefits

The ideal shade tree has a fairly dense, round crown with limbs broad enough to partially shade the roof. Given the same placement, a large tree will provide more shade than a small tree. Deciduous trees allow sun to shine through leafless branches in winter. Plant small trees where nearby buildings or power lines limit aboveground space. Columnar trees are appropriate in narrow side yards. Because the best location for shade trees is relatively close to the west and east sides of buildings, the most suitable trees will be strong and capable of resisting storm damage, disease, and pests (Sand 1994). Examples of trees not to select for placement near buildings include cottonwoods (**Populus** spp.) and silver maple (**Acer saccharinum**) because their invasive roots, weak wood, and large size, and ginkgos (**Ginkgo biloba**) because of their sparse shade and slow growth.

When selecting trees, match the tree's water requirements with those of surrounding plants. For instance, select low water-use species for planting in areas that receive little irrigation. Also, match the tree's maintenance requirements with the amount of care and the type of use different areas in the landscape receive. For instance, tree species that drop fruit that can be a slip-and-fall problem should not be planted near paved areas that are frequently used by pedestrians. Check with your local landscape professional before selecting trees to make sure that they are well suited to the site's soil and climatic conditions.

Use the following practices to plant and manage trees strategically to maximize energy conservation benefits:

- Increase community-wide tree canopy, and target shade to streets, parking lots, and other paved surfaces, as well as air-conditioned buildings.

- Shade west- and east-facing windows and walls.

- Avoid planting trees to the south of buildings.

- Select solar-friendly trees opposite east- and south-facing walls.

- Shade air conditioners, but don't obstruct air flow.

- Avoid planting trees too close to utilities and buildings.

- Create multi-row, evergreen windbreaks where space permits, that are longer than the building.

*Select trees well suited to the site*

## *Guidelines for Reducing Carbon Dioxide*

Because trees in common areas and other public places may not shelter buildings from sun and wind and reduce energy use, $CO_2$ reductions are primarily due to sequestration. Fast-growing trees sequester more $CO_2$ initially than slow-growing trees, but this advantage can be lost if the fast-growing trees die at younger ages. Large trees have the capacity to store more $CO_2$ than smaller trees (**Figure 28**). To maximize $CO_2$ sequestration, select tree species that are well suited to the site where they will be planted. Consult with your local landscape professional or arborist to select the right tree for your site. Trees that are not well adapted will grow slowly, show symptoms of stress, or die at an early age. Unhealthy trees do little to reduce atmospheric $CO_2$ and can be unsightly liabilities in the landscape.

*Figure 28. Compared with small trees, large trees can store more carbon, filter more air pollutants, intercept more rainfall, and provide greater energy savings.*

Design and management guidelines that can increase $CO_2$ reductions include the following:

- Maximize use of woody plants, especially trees, as they store more $CO_2$ than do herbaceous plants and grasses.

- Plant more trees where feasible and immediately replace dead trees to compensate for $CO_2$ lost through tree and stump removal.

- Create a diverse assemblage of habitats, with trees of different ages and species, to promote a continuous canopy cover over time.

- Group species with similar landscape maintenance requirements together and consider how irrigation, pruning, fertilization, weed, pest, and disease control can be minimized.

- Reduce $CO_2$ associated with landscape management by using push mowers (not gas or electric), hand saws (not chain saws), pruners (not gas/electric shears), rakes (not leaf blowers), and employ landscape professionals who don't have to travel far to your site.

- Reduce maintenance by reducing turfgrass and planting drought-tolerant or environmentally friendly landscapes.

- Consider the project's life span when selecting species. Fast-growing species will sequester more $CO_2$ initially than slow-growing species, but may not live as long.

- Provide ample space belowground for tree roots to grow so that they can maximize $CO_2$ sequestration and tree longevity.

- When trees die or are removed, salvage as much wood as possible for use as furniture and other long-lasting products to delay decomposition.

- Plant trees, shrubs, and vines in strategic locations to maximize summer shade and reduce winter shade, thereby reducing atmospheric $CO_2$ emissions associated with power production.

*Maximizing bioretention by trees*

*Figure 29. Tree can create a continuous canopy for maximum rainfall interception, even in commercial areas. In this example, a swale in the median filters runoff and provides ample space for large trees. Parking space-sized planters contain the soil volume required to grow healthy, large trees (from Metro 2002).*

## *Guidelines for Reducing Storm-water Runoff*

Trees are mini-reservoirs, controlling runoff at the source because their leaves and branch surfaces intercept and store rainfall, thereby reducing runoff volumes and erosion of watercourses, as well as delaying the onset of peak flows. Rainfall interception by large trees is a relatively inexpensive first line of defense in the battle to control nonpoint-source pollution.

When selecting trees to maximize rainfall interception benefits:

- Select tree species with architectural features that maximize interception, such as large **leaf surface area** and rough surfaces that store water (Metro 2002).

- Increase interception by planting

large trees where possible (**Figure 29**).

- Plant trees that are in leaf when precipitation is greatest.

- Select conifers because they have high interception rates, but avoid shading south-facing windows to maximize solar heat gain in winter.

- Plant low-water-use tree species where appropriate and native species that, once established, require little supplemental irrigation.

- In bioretention areas, such as roadside swales, select species that tolerate inundation, are long-lived, wide-spreading, and fast-growing (Metro 2002).

- Do not pave over streetside planting strips for easier weed control; this can reduce tree health and increase runoff.

## *Guidelines for Improving Air Quality Benefits*

Trees, sometimes called the "lungs of our cities," are important because of their ability to remove contaminants from the air. The amount of gaseous pollutants and particulates removed by trees depends on their size and architecture, as well as local meteorology and pollutant concentrations.

Along streets, in parking lots, and in commercial areas locate trees to maximize shade on paving and parked vehicles. Shade trees reduce heat that is stored or reflected by paved surfaces. By cooling streets and parking areas, trees reduce emissions of evaporative hydrocarbons from parked cars and thereby reduce smog formation (Scott et al. 1999). Large trees can shade a greater area than smaller trees, but should be used only where space permits. Remember that a tree needs space for both branches and roots.

Tree planting and management guidelines to improve air quality include the following (Smith and Dochinger 1976; Nowak 2000):

- Select species that tolerate pollutants that are present in harmful concentrations. For example, in areas with high $O_3$ concentration avoid sensitive species such as white and green ash (**Fraxinus americana** and **F. pennsylvanica**), tulip tree (**Liriodendron tulipifera**), and Austrian pine (**Pinus nigra**) (Noble et al. 1988).

- Conifers have high surface-to-volume ratios and retain their foliage year-round, which may make them more effective than deciduous species.

- Species with long leaf stems (e.g., ash, maple) and hairy plant parts (e.g., oak, birch, sumac) are especially efficient interceptors.

- Effective uptake depends on proximity to the pollutant source and the amount of biomass. Where space permits, plant multi-layered stands near the source of pollutants.

- Consider the local meteorology and topography to promote air flow that can "flush" pollutants at night and avoid trapping them in the urban canopy layer during the day.

- In areas with unhealthy ozone concentrations, maximize use of plants that emit low levels of BVOCs to reduce ozone formation.

- Sustain large, healthy trees; they produce the most benefits.

- To reduce emissions of VOCs and other pollutants, plant trees to shade parked cars and conserve energy.

- In polluted or heavily populated areas, plant trees that tolerate pollution.

## *Avoiding Tree Conflicts with Infrastructure*

- Before planting, contact your local before-digging company, such as One-Call Center, Inc., or Miss Utility, to locate underground water, sewer, gas, and telecommunications lines.

- Avoid locating trees where they will block streetlights or views of traffic and commercial signs.

- Check with local transportation officials for sight visibility requirements. Keep trees at least 30 ft (10 m) away from street intersections to ensure visibility.

- Avoid planting shallow-rooting species near sidewalks, curbs, and paving to reduce sidewalk heave by roots. Generally, avoid planting within 3 ft (1 m) of pavement, and remember that trunk flare at the base of large trees can displace soil and paving for a considerable distance. Consider strategies to reduce infrastructure damage by tree roots such as meandering sidewalks around trees and planting deep-rooting species (Costello and Jones 2003).

- Select small trees (<25 ft tall [8 m]) for location under overhead power lines, and do not plant directly above un-

*Figure 30. (a,b) Know where power lines and other utility lines are before planting. (c) Under power lines use only small-growing trees ("low zone") and avoid planting directly above underground utilities. Larger trees may be planted where space permits ("medium" and "tall zones") (from ISA 1992).*

derground water and sewer lines (**Figure 30**). Avoid locating trees where they will block illumination from streetlights or views of street signs in parking lots, commercial areas, and along streets.

*Match each tree to its site*

For trees to deliver benefits over the long term they require enough soil volume to grow and remain healthy. Matching tree species to the site's soil volume can reduce sidewalk and curb damage as well. **Figure 31** shows recommended soil volumes for different sized trees.

Maintenance requirements and public safety issues influence the type of trees selected for public places. The ideal public tree is not susceptible to wind damage and branch drop, does not require frequent pruning, produces negligible litter, is deep-rooted, has few serious pest and disease problems, and tolerates a wide range of soil conditions, irrigation regimes, and air pollutants. Because relatively few

## SOIL VOLUME FOR TREES

Figure 31. Developed from several sources by Urban (1992), this graph shows the relationship between tree size and required soil volume. For example, a tree with a 16-inch diameter at breast height (41 cm) with 640 ft² of crown projection area (59.5 m² under the dripline) requires 1,000 ft³ (28 m³) of soil (from Costello and Jones 2003).

trees have all these traits, it is important to match the tree species to the planting site by determining what issues are most important on a case-by-case basis. For example, parking-lot trees should be tolerant of hot, dry conditions, have strong branch attachments, and be resistant to attacks by pests that leave vehicles covered with sticky exudates. Check with your local landscape professional for horticultural information on tree traits.

*The root ball is critical to survival*

### General Guidelines to Maximize Long-Term Benefits

Selecting a tree from the nursery that has a high probability of becoming a healthy, trouble-free **mature tree** is critical to a successful outcome. Therefore, select the very best stock at your nursery, and when necessary, reject nursery stock that does not meet industry standards.

*A good tree is well anchored*

The health of the tree's root ball is critical to its ultimate survival. If the tree is in a container, check for matted roots by sliding off the container. Roots should penetrate to the edge of the root ball, but not densely circle the inside of the container or grow through drain holes. As well, at least two large structural roots should emerge from the trunk within 1–3 inches of the soil surface. If there are no roots in the upper portion of the root ball, it is undersized and the tree should not be planted.

Another way to evaluate the quality of the tree before planting is to gently move the trunk back and forth. A good tree trunk bends and does not move in the soil, while a poor trunk bends a little and pivots at or below the soil line—a tell-tale sign of a poorly anchored tree.

Dig the planting hole 1 inch shallower than the depth of the root ball to allow for some settling after watering. Make the hole two to three

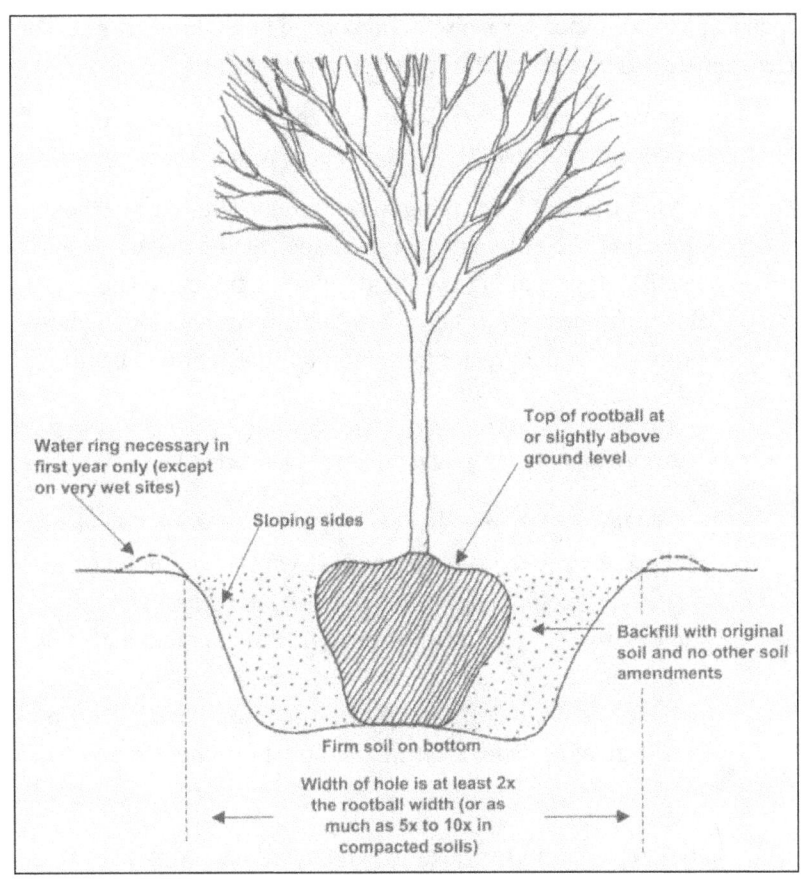

Figure 32. Prepare a broad planting area, plant the tree with the root flare at ground level, and provide a berm/water ring to retain water (from Head et al. 2001).

times as wide as the root ball and loosen the sides of the hole to make it easier for roots to penetrate. Place the tree so that the root flare is at the top of the soil. If the structural roots have grown properly as described above, the top of the root ball will be slightly higher (1–2 inches) than the surrounding soil to allow for settling. Backfill with the native soil unless it is very rocky or sandy, in which case you may want to add composted organic matter such as peat moss or shredded bark (**Figure 32**).

Planting trees in urban plazas, commercial areas, and parking lots poses special challenges due to limited soil volume and poor soil structure. Engineered or structural soils can be placed under the hardscape to increase rooting space while meeting engineering requirements. For more information on structural soils see **Reducing Infrastructure Damage by Tree Roots: A Compendium of Strategies** (Costello and Jones 2003).

*Mulch and water*

Use the extra soil left after planting to build a berm outside the root ball that is 6 in (15 cm) high and 3 ft (1 m) in diameter. Soak the tree, and gently rock it to settle it in. Cover the basin with a 2- to 4-in (10-cm) thick layer of mulch, but avoid placing mulch against the tree trunk. Water the new tree three times a week and increase the amount of water as the tree grows larger. Generally, a tree requires about 1

*Don't forget about the tree*

inch (2.5 cm) of water per week. A rain gauge or soil moisture sensor (tensiometer) can help determine tree watering needs.

- Inspect your tree several times a year, and contact a local landscape professional if problems develop.

- If your tree needed staking to keep it upright, remove the stake and ties after one year or as soon as the tree can hold itself up. The staking should allow some tree movement, as this movement sends hormones to the roots causing them to grow and create greater tree stability. It also promotes trunk taper and growth.

- Reapply mulch and irrigate the tree as needed.

*Additional resources*

- Leave lower side branches on young trees for the first year and prune back to 4–6 inches (10–15 cm) to accelerate tree diameter development. Remove these lateral branches after the first full year. Prune the young tree to maintain a central main trunk and equally spaced branches. For more information, see Costello 2000. As the tree matures, have it pruned on a regular basis by a certified arborist or other experienced professional.

- By keeping your tree healthy, you maximize its ability to produce shade, intercept rainfall, reduce atmospheric $CO_2$, and provide other benefits. For additional information on tree selection, planting, establishment, and care see the following resources:

  - The **Urban Forestry Manual** and other resources available at www.urbanforestry south.org and supported by the USDA Forest Service, Southern Region.

  - **Tree City USA Bulletin** series (Fazio, undated), International Society of Arboriculture (ISA) brochures (www.isa-arbor.com and www.treesaregood.com)

  - **Native Trees, Shrubs, and Vines for Urban and Rural America** (Hightshoe 1988)

  - **Principles and Practice of Planting Trees and Shrubs** (Watson and Himelick 1997)

  - **Arboriculture** (Harris et al. 1999)

  - **Training Young Trees for Structure and Form** (Costello 2000) video

  - **Trees for Urban and Suburban Landscapes** (Gil-

# *Appendix A: Benefit–Cost Information Tables*

Information in this Appendix can be used to estimate benefits and costs associated with proposed tree plantings. The tables contain data for representative large (**Acer rubrum**, red maple), medium (**Magnolia grandiflora**, Southern magnolia), and small (**Cornus florida**, dogwood) broadleaf trees and a representative conifer (**Pinus taeda**, loblolly pine). Data are presented as annual values for each 5-year interval after planting (**Tables A1–A3**). Annual values incorporate effects of tree loss. Based on the results of our survey, we assume that 45% of the trees planted die by the end of the 40-year period.

The tables are divided into three sections: benefits, costs, and net benefits. For the benefits section of the tables, there are two columns for each 5-year interval. In the first column, values describe **resource units** (RUs): for example, the amount of air conditioning energy saved in kWh per year per tree, air pollutant uptake in pounds per year per tree, and rainfall intercepted in gallons per year per tree. Energy and $CO_2$ benefits for residential yard trees are broken out by tree location to show how shading impacts vary among trees opposite west-, south-, and east-facing building walls. The second column for each 5-year interval contains dollar values obtained by multiplying RUs by local prices (e.g., kWh saved [RU] x $/kWh).

In the second section of the tables, costs are broken down into categories for yard and public trees. Costs for yard trees do not vary by planting location (i.e., east, west, south walls). Although tree and planting costs occur at year one, we divided this value by five years to derive an average annual cost for the first 5-year period. All other costs are the estimated values for each year and not values averaged over five years.

In the third section of the tables, total net benefits are calculated by subtracting total costs from total benefits. Data are presented for a yard tree opposite west-, south-, and east-facing walls, as well as for the public tree.

The last column in each table presents 40-year-average annual values. These numbers were calculated by dividing the total costs and benefits by 40 years.

**Table A1. Annual benefits, costs and net benefits at 5-year intervals and 40-year averages for a representative large broadleaf tree (red maple, Acer rubrum)**

| Benefits/tree | Year 5 RU | Year 5 $ | Year 10 RU | Year 10 $ | Year 15 RU | Year 15 $ | Year 20 RU | Year 20 $ | Year 25 RU | Year 25 $ | Year 30 RU | Year 30 $ | Year 35 RU | Year 35 $ | Year 40 RU | Year 40 $ | 40-year average RU | 40-year average $ |
|---|---|---|---|---|---|---|---|---|---|---|---|---|---|---|---|---|---|---|
| **Cooling (kWh)** | | | | | | | | | | | | | | | | | | |
| Yard: West | 33 | 2 54 | 100 | 7 59 | 168 | 12 76 | 224 | 16 99 | 274 | 20 83 | 313 | 23 74 | 345 | 26 22 | 276 | 20 94 | 217 | 16 45 |
| Yard: South | 11 | 0 84 | 39 | 2 94 | 76 | 5 74 | 115 | 8 74 | 161 | 12 20 | 201 | 15 29 | 243 | 18 45 | 250 | 18 96 | 137 | 10 39 |
| Yard: East | 22 | 1 68 | 72 | 5 50 | 127 | 9 62 | 174 | 13 19 | 219 | 16 65 | 255 | 19 33 | 284 | 21 52 | 248 | 18 80 | 175 | 13 29 |
| Public | 10 | 0 75 | 28 | 2 10 | 49 | 3 70 | 69 | 5 25 | 98 | 7 43 | 125 | 9 50 | 154 | 11 68 | 178 | 13 50 | 89 | 6 74 |
| **Heating (kBtu)** | | | | | | | | | | | | | | | | | | |
| Yard: West | 73 | 0 77 | 171 | 1 79 | 275 | 2 87 | 363 | 3 80 | 436 | 4 56 | 485 | 5 07 | 517 | 5 40 | 552 | 5 77 | 359 | 3 75 |
| Yard: South | 42 | 0 44 | 47 | 0 49 | 73 | 0 76 | 117 | 1 23 | 169 | 1 77 | 214 | 2 24 | 249 | 2 61 | 423 | 4 42 | 167 | 1 74 |
| Yard: East | 56 | 0 58 | 138 | 1 45 | 233 | 2 44 | 321 | 3 35 | 397 | 4 15 | 451 | 4 71 | 485 | 5 07 | 544 | 5 69 | 328 | 3 43 |
| Public | 88 | 0 92 | 201 | 2 11 | 320 | 3 35 | 421 | 4 40 | 507 | 5 30 | 566 | 5 92 | 603 | 6 31 | 613 | 6 41 | 415 | 4 34 |
| **Net energy (kBtu)** | | | | | | | | | | | | | | | | | | |
| Yard: West | 408 | 3 31 | 1171 | 9 38 | 1956 | 15 64 | 2601 | 20 79 | 3180 | 25 39 | 3613 | 28 81 | 3971 | 31 63 | 3310 | 26 71 | 2526 | 20 21 |
| Yard: South | 152 | 1 27 | 435 | 3 44 | 830 | 6 51 | 1268 | 9 96 | 1777 | 13 97 | 2228 | 17 52 | 2680 | 21 05 | 2920 | 23 38 | 1536 | 12 14 |
| Yard: East | 277 | 2 26 | 863 | 6 94 | 1500 | 12 05 | 2059 | 16 55 | 2590 | 20 80 | 2998 | 24 04 | 3321 | 26 60 | 3021 | 24 49 | 2078 | 16 72 |
| Public | 187 | 1 67 | 478 | 4 21 | 808 | 7 05 | 1112 | 9 65 | 1485 | 12 73 | 1818 | 15 42 | 2142 | 17 99 | 2392 | 19 91 | 1303 | 11 08 |
| **Net CO$_2$ (lb)** | | | | | | | | | | | | | | | | | | |
| Yard: West | 58 | 0 43 | 152 | 1 14 | 263 | 1 97 | 371 | 2 78 | 497 | 3 73 | 618 | 4 63 | 757 | 5 68 | 815 | 6 12 | 441 | 3 31 |
| Yard: South | 35 | 0 26 | 86 | 0 64 | 161 | 1 21 | 250 | 1 88 | 370 | 2 77 | 492 | 3 69 | 639 | 4 79 | 778 | 5 84 | 351 | 2 64 |
| Yard: East | 46 | 0 35 | 125 | 0 94 | 223 | 1 67 | 324 | 2 43 | 446 | 3 34 | 565 | 4 24 | 701 | 5 26 | 791 | 5 93 | 403 | 3 02 |
| Public | 40 | 0 30 | 94 | 0 71 | 167 | 1 25 | 247 | 1 85 | 356 | 2 67 | 469 | 3 52 | 605 | 4 54 | 740 | 5 55 | 340 | 2 55 |
| **Air pollution (lb)** | | | | | | | | | | | | | | | | | | |
| O$_3$ uptake | 0 02 | 0 14 | 0 06 | 0 38 | 0 11 | 0 69 | 0 16 | 1 04 | 0 23 | 1 48 | 0 29 | 1 93 | 0 38 | 2 46 | 0 46 | 2 99 | 0 21 | 1 39 |
| NO$_2$ uptake+avoided | 0 05 | 0 34 | 0 15 | 1 00 | 0 27 | 1 76 | 0 38 | 2 46 | 0 49 | 3 22 | 0 59 | 3 87 | 0 69 | 4 51 | 0 69 | 4 51 | 0 41 | 2 71 |
| SO$_2$ uptake+avoided | 0 10 | 0 19 | 0 31 | 0 60 | 0 55 | 1 06 | 0 77 | 1 47 | 1 00 | 1 91 | 1 19 | 2 28 | 1 37 | 2 62 | 1 29 | 2 46 | 0 82 | 1 57 |
| PM$_{10}$ uptake+avoided | 0 01 | 0 02 | 0 05 | 0 11 | 0 12 | 0 28 | 0 23 | 0 53 | 0 35 | 0 80 | 0 46 | 1 07 | 0 58 | 1 34 | 0 68 | 1 56 | 0 31 | 0 71 |
| VOCs avoided | 0 01 | 0 05 | 0 03 | 0 17 | 0 05 | 0 29 | 0 06 | 0 40 | 0 08 | 0 52 | 0 10 | 0 62 | 0 11 | 0 71 | 0 11 | 0 66 | 0 07 | 0 43 |
| BVOCs released | -0 00 | -0 01 | -0 00 | -0 03 | -0 06 | -0 40 | -0 23 | -1 43 | -0 46 | -2 84 | -0 72 | -4 46 | -0 98 | -6 08 | -1 21 | -7 53 | -0 46 | -2 85 |
| Avoided + net uptake | 0 19 | 0 74 | 0 59 | 2 23 | 1 03 | 3 67 | 1 37 | 4 48 | 1 69 | 5 08 | 1 92 | 5 31 | 2 15 | 5 56 | 2 01 | 4 66 | 1 37 | 3 97 |
| **Hydrology (gal)** | | | | | | | | | | | | | | | | | | |
| Rainfall interception | 185 | 1 83 | 793 | 7 85 | 1,784 | 17 66 | 3,067 | 30 36 | 4,854 | 48 05 | 6,788 | 67 20 | 9,177 | 90 85 | 11,577 | 114 61 | 4,778 | 47 30 |
| **Aesthetics and other benefits** | | | | | | | | | | | | | | | | | | |
| Yard | | 0 99 | | 17 92 | | 28 80 | | 38 75 | | 46 92 | | 52 51 | | 54 79 | | 53 15 | | 36 73 |
| Public | | 1 11 | | 20 02 | | 32 17 | | 43 28 | | 52 41 | | 58 65 | | 61 19 | | 59 36 | | 41 02 |
| **Total Benefits** | | | | | | | | | | | | | | | | | | |
| Yard: West | | 7 31 | | 38 52 | | 67 74 | | 97 15 | | 129 17 | | 158 47 | | 188 50 | | 205 24 | | 111 51 |
| Yard: South | | 5 11 | | 32 08 | | 57 84 | | 85 43 | | 116 80 | | 146 23 | | 177 04 | | 201 63 | | 102 77 |
| Yard: East | | 6 18 | | 35 88 | | 63 85 | | 92 56 | | 124 19 | | 153 30 | | 183 05 | | 202 84 | | 107 73 |
| Public | | 5 65 | | 35 01 | | 61 80 | | 89 62 | | 120 94 | | 150 10 | | 180 13 | | 204 09 | | 105 92 |
| **Costs ($/year/tree)** | | | | | | | | | | | | | | | | | | |
| **Tree & planting** | | | | | | | | | | | | | | | | | | |
| Yard | | 100 00 | | | | | | | | | | | | | | | | 12 50 |
| Public | | 44 00 | | | | | | | | | | | | | | | | 5 50 |
| **Pruning** | | | | | | | | | | | | | | | | | | |
| Yard | | 2 82 | | 2 78 | | 2 73 | | 4 21 | | 4 14 | | 4 07 | | 4 01 | | 3 94 | | 3 33 |
| Public | | 9 45 | | 8 93 | | 8 40 | | 9 60 | | 8 96 | | 8 32 | | 7 68 | | 7 04 | | 8 34 |
| **Remove & dispose** | | | | | | | | | | | | | | | | | | |
| Yard | | 1 79 | | 0 72 | | 1 04 | | 1 38 | | 1 75 | | 2 15 | | 2 58 | | 3 03 | | 1 59 |
| Public | | 2 99 | | 2 51 | | 3 62 | | 4 83 | | 6 14 | | 7 54 | | 9 03 | | 10 62 | | 5 32 |
| **Pest & Disease** | | | | | | | | | | | | | | | | | | |
| Yard | | 0 35 | | 0 58 | | 0 83 | | 1 09 | | 1 36 | | 1 64 | | 1 94 | | 2 24 | | 1 15 |
| Public | | 0 00 | | 0 00 | | 0 00 | | 0 00 | | 0 01 | | 0 01 | | 0 01 | | 0 01 | | 0 00 |
| **Infrastructure repair** | | | | | | | | | | | | | | | | | | |
| Yard | | 0 20 | | 0 32 | | 0 46 | | 0 60 | | 0 75 | | 0 91 | | 1 07 | | 1 24 | | 0 64 |
| Public | | 1 50 | | 2 37 | | 3 22 | | 4 03 | | 4 78 | | 5 45 | | 6 02 | | 6 50 | | 3 95 |
| **Irrigation** | | | | | | | | | | | | | | | | | | |
| Yard | | 0 00 | | 0 00 | | 0 00 | | 0 00 | | 0 00 | | 0 00 | | 0 00 | | 0 00 | | 0 00 |
| Public | | 0 00 | | 0 00 | | 0 00 | | 0 00 | | 0 00 | | 0 00 | | 0 00 | | 0 00 | | 0 00 |
| **Clean-Up** | | | | | | | | | | | | | | | | | | |
| Yard | | 0 02 | | 0 04 | | 0 05 | | 0 07 | | 0 08 | | 0 10 | | 0 12 | | 0 14 | | 0 07 |
| Public | | 0 17 | | 0 26 | | 0 36 | | 0 45 | | 0 53 | | 0 61 | | 0 67 | | 0 72 | | 0 44 |
| **Liabiity & Legal** | | | | | | | | | | | | | | | | | | |
| Yard | | 0 02 | | 0 04 | | 0 05 | | 0 07 | | 0 08 | | 0 10 | | 0 12 | | 0 14 | | 0 07 |
| Public | | 0 16 | | 0 26 | | 0 35 | | 0 44 | | 0 52 | | 0 59 | | 0 66 | | 0 71 | | 0 43 |
| **Admin/inspect/other** | | | | | | | | | | | | | | | | | | |
| Yard | | 0 00 | | 0 00 | | 0 00 | | 0 00 | | 0 00 | | 0 00 | | 0 00 | | 0 00 | | 0 00 |
| Public | | 1 11 | | 1 75 | | 2 38 | | 2 98 | | 3 53 | | 4 03 | | 4 45 | | 4 80 | | 2 92 |
| **Total costs** | | | | | | | | | | | | | | | | | | |
| Yard | | 105 20 | | 4 47 | | 5 16 | | 7 41 | | 8 17 | | 8 98 | | 9 83 | | 10 73 | | 19 35 |
| Public | | 59 37 | | 16 09 | | 18 34 | | 22 33 | | 24 46 | | 26 53 | | 28 52 | | 30 39 | | 26 89 |
| **Total net benefits** | | | | | | | | | | | | | | | | | | |
| Yard: West | | -98 | | 34 | | 63 | | 90 | | 121 | | 149 | | 179 | | 195 | | 92 |
| Yard: South | | -100 | | 28 | | 53 | | 78 | | 109 | | 137 | | 167 | | 191 | | 83 |
| Yard: East | | -99 | | 31 | | 59 | | 85 | | 116 | | 144 | | 173 | | 192 | | 88 |
| Public | | -54 | | 19 | | 43 | | 67 | | 96 | | 124 | | 152 | | 174 | | 79 |

## Table A2. Annual benefits, costs and net benefits at 5-year intervals and 40-year averages for a representative medium broadleaf tree (Southern magnolia, *Magnolia grandiflora*)

| Benefits/tree | Year 5 RU | Year 5 $ | Year 10 RU | Year 10 $ | Year 15 RU | Year 15 $ | Year 20 RU | Year 20 $ | Year 25 RU | Year 25 $ | Year 30 RU | Year 30 $ | Year 35 RU | Year 35 $ | Year 40 RU | Year 40 $ | 40-year average RU | 40-year average $ |
|---|---|---|---|---|---|---|---|---|---|---|---|---|---|---|---|---|---|---|
| **Cooling (kWh)** | | | | | | | | | | | | | | | | | | |
| Yard: West | 16 | 1 24 | 47 | 3 53 | 96 | 7 26 | 143 | 10 85 | 190 | 14 43 | 229 | 17 37 | 264 | 20 05 | 295 | 22 38 | 160 | 12 14 |
| Yard: South | 8 | 0 61 | 20 | 1 50 | 40 | 3 05 | 67 | 5 08 | 96 | 7 28 | 129 | 9 78 | 163 | 12 36 | 199 | 15 11 | 90 | 6 85 |
| Yard: East | 11 | 0 86 | 31 | 2 32 | 62 | 4 72 | 97 | 7 32 | 132 | 10 02 | 166 | 12 59 | 199 | 15 08 | 226 | 17 15 | 115 | 8 76 |
| Public | 7 | 0 56 | 15 | 1 15 | 27 | 2 01 | 40 | 3 01 | 53 | 4 05 | 71 | 5 42 | 91 | 6 88 | 116 | 8 81 | 53 | 3 99 |
| **Heating (kBtu)** | | | | | | | | | | | | | | | | | | |
| Yard: West | 57 | 0 59 | 75 | 0 79 | 95 | 1 00 | 121 | 1 26 | 148 | 1 55 | 172 | 1 80 | 193 | 2 02 | 202 | 2 11 | 133 | 1 39 |
| Yard: South | 33 | 0 35 | -46 | -0 48 | -216 | -2 26 | -384 | -4 01 | -553 | -5 78 | -655 | -6 85 | -733 | -7 67 | -758 | -7 93 | -414 | -4 33 |
| Yard: East | 35 | 0 37 | 18 | 0 19 | -6 | -0 07 | -3 | -0 03 | 9 | 0 09 | 27 | 0 29 | 48 | 0 50 | 64 | 0 67 | 24 | 0 25 |
| Public | 76 | 0 79 | 130 | 1 36 | 198 | 2 07 | 269 | 2 81 | 342 | 3 57 | 405 | 4 23 | 463 | 4 85 | 500 | 5 23 | 298 | 3 12 |
| **Net energy (kBtu)** | | | | | | | | | | | | | | | | | | |
| Yard: West | 220 | 1 83 | 541 | 4 32 | 1052 | 8 26 | 1551 | 12 12 | 2050 | 15 98 | 2461 | 19 17 | 2835 | 22 07 | 3151 | 24 49 | 1733 | 13 53 |
| Yard: South | 113 | 0 95 | 152 | 1 02 | 186 | 0 79 | 285 | 1 06 | 406 | 1 49 | 634 | 2 93 | 896 | 4 70 | 1233 | 7 18 | 488 | 2 52 |
| Yard: East | 149 | 1 23 | 323 | 2 50 | 615 | 4 65 | 962 | 7 29 | 1329 | 10 11 | 1686 | 12 88 | 2035 | 15 58 | 2324 | 17 82 | 1178 | 9 01 |
| Public | 149 | 1 35 | 281 | 2 51 | 463 | 4 08 | 665 | 5 82 | 876 | 7 63 | 1119 | 9 65 | 1370 | 11 73 | 1662 | 14 05 | 823 | 7 10 |
| **Net $CO_2$ (lb)** | | | | | | | | | | | | | | | | | | |
| Yard: West | 23 | 0 17 | 57 | 0 43 | 110 | 0 83 | 167 | 1 25 | 226 | 1 70 | 282 | 2 11 | 337 | 2 53 | 395 | 2 96 | 200 | 1 50 |
| Yard: South | 13 | 0 10 | 20 | 0 15 | 27 | 0 20 | 43 | 0 32 | 64 | 0 48 | 100 | 0 75 | 143 | 1 07 | 201 | 1 51 | 76 | 0 57 |
| Yard: East | 16 | 0 12 | 37 | 0 27 | 70 | 0 52 | 113 | 0 85 | 161 | 1 21 | 212 | 1 59 | 265 | 1 99 | 320 | 2 40 | 149 | 1 12 |
| Public | 18 | 0 13 | 37 | 0 28 | 64 | 0 48 | 97 | 0 73 | 133 | 1 00 | 176 | 1 32 | 223 | 1 67 | 279 | 2 09 | 128 | 0 96 |
| **Air pollution (lb)** | | | | | | | | | | | | | | | | | | |
| $O_3$ uptake | 0 05 | 0 31 | 0 09 | 0 59 | 0 15 | 0 99 | 0 24 | 1 55 | 0 34 | 2 22 | 0 47 | 3 07 | 0 62 | 4 09 | 0 82 | 5 35 | 0 35 | 2 27 |
| $NO_2$ uptake+avoided | 0 04 | 0 28 | 0 09 | 0 59 | 0 16 | 1 08 | 0 25 | 1 65 | 0 35 | 2 27 | 0 45 | 2 96 | 0 57 | 3 70 | 0 69 | 4 53 | 0 33 | 2 13 |
| $SO_2$ uptake+avoided | 0 06 | 0 12 | 0 16 | 0 31 | 0 32 | 0 61 | 0 49 | 0 94 | 0 67 | 1 28 | 0 85 | 1 63 | 1 04 | 1 99 | 1 23 | 2 35 | 0 60 | 1 15 |
| $PM_{10}$ uptake+avoided | 0 02 | 0 06 | 0 06 | 0 14 | 0 15 | 0 34 | 0 30 | 0 70 | 0 52 | 1 20 | 0 79 | 1 83 | 1 12 | 2 58 | 1 50 | 3 46 | 0 56 | 1 29 |
| VOCs avoided | 0 01 | 0 03 | 0 01 | 0 08 | 0 02 | 0 15 | 0 04 | 0 23 | 0 05 | 0 32 | 0 06 | 0 40 | 0 08 | 0 48 | 0 09 | 0 56 | 0 05 | 0 28 |
| BVOCs released | -0 01 | -0 04 | -0 02 | -0 15 | -0 22 | -1 37 | -0 67 | -4 15 | -1 22 | -7 58 | -1 75 | -10 93 | -2 16 | -13 47 | -2 32 | -14 48 | -1 05 | -6 52 |
| Avoided + net uptake | 0 18 | 0 75 | 0 39 | 1 57 | 0 58 | 1 80 | 0 65 | 0 91 | 0 71 | -0 30 | 0 87 | -1 04 | 1 26 | -0 63 | 2 00 | 1 78 | 0 83 | 0 61 |
| **Hydrology (gal)** | | | | | | | | | | | | | | | | | | |
| Rainfall interception | 160 | 1 59 | 419 | 4 15 | 920 | 9 10 | 1,656 | 16 39 | 2,560 | 25 34 | 3,646 | 36 09 | 4,910 | 48 61 | 6,257 | 61 95 | 2,566 | 25 40 |
| **Aesthetics and other benefits** | | | | | | | | | | | | | | | | | | |
| Yard | | 0 60 | | 6 42 | | 10 34 | | 13 51 | | 15 75 | | 16 93 | | 16 96 | | 15 77 | | 12 03 |
| Public | | 0 67 | | 7 17 | | 11 55 | | 15 09 | | 17 59 | | 18 91 | | 18 94 | | 17 62 | | 13 44 |
| **Total benefits** | | | | | | | | | | | | | | | | | | |
| Yard: West | | 4 94 | | 16 88 | | 30 33 | | 44 18 | | 58 48 | | 73 27 | | 89 54 | | 106 96 | | 53 07 |
| Yard: South | | 3 99 | | 13 30 | | 22 23 | | 32 20 | | 42 77 | | 55 67 | | 70 71 | | 88 19 | | 41 13 |
| Yard: East | | 4 29 | | 14 91 | | 26 42 | | 38 96 | | 52 11 | | 66 45 | | 82 51 | | 99 73 | | 48 17 |
| Public | | 4 49 | | 15 66 | | 27 02 | | 38 95 | | 51 27 | | 64 94 | | 80 32 | | 97 49 | | 47 52 |
| **Costs ($/year/tree)** | | | | | | | | | | | | | | | | | | |
| **Tree & planting** | | | | | | | | | | | | | | | | | | |
| Yard | | 100 00 | | | | | | | | | | | | | | | | 12 50 |
| Public | | 44 00 | | | | | | | | | | | | | | | | 5 50 |
| **Pruning** | | | | | | | | | | | | | | | | | | |
| Yard | | 0 06 | | 2 78 | | 2 73 | | 2 69 | | 2 65 | | 4 07 | | 4 01 | | 3 94 | | 2 61 |
| Public | | 4 95 | | 8 93 | | 8 40 | | 7 88 | | 7 35 | | 8 32 | | 7 68 | | 7 04 | | 7 65 |
| **Remove & dispose** | | | | | | | | | | | | | | | | | | |
| Yard | | 1 42 | | 0 60 | | 0 87 | | 1 16 | | 1 46 | | 1 77 | | 2 10 | | 2 45 | | 1 29 |
| Public | | 1 06 | | 2 09 | | 3 04 | | 4 05 | | 5 10 | | 6 20 | | 7 36 | | 8 56 | | 4 29 |
| **Pest & disease** | | | | | | | | | | | | | | | | | | |
| Yard | | 0 28 | | 0 49 | | 0 70 | | 0 91 | | 1 13 | | 1 35 | | 1 58 | | 1 81 | | 0 94 |
| Public | | 0 00 | | 0 00 | | 0 00 | | 0 00 | | 0 00 | | 0 01 | | 0 01 | | 0 01 | | 0 00 |
| **Infrastructure repair** | | | | | | | | | | | | | | | | | | |
| Yard | | 0 16 | | 0 27 | | 0 39 | | 0 50 | | 0 63 | | 0 75 | | 0 67 | | 1 00 | | 0 52 |
| Public | | 1 19 | | 1 98 | | 2 71 | | 3 38 | | 3 97 | | 4 48 | | 4 91 | | 5 23 | | 3 24 |
| **Irrigation** | | | | | | | | | | | | | | | | | | |
| Yard | | 0 00 | | 0 00 | | 0 00 | | 0 00 | | 0 00 | | 0 00 | | 0 00 | | 0 00 | | 0 00 |
| Public | | 0 00 | | 0 00 | | 0 00 | | 0 00 | | 0 00 | | 0 00 | | 0 00 | | 0 00 | | 0 00 |
| **Clean-Up** | | | | | | | | | | | | | | | | | | |
| Yard | | 0 02 | | 0 03 | | 0 04 | | 0 06 | | 0 07 | | 0 08 | | 0 08 | | 0 11 | | 0 06 |
| Public | | 0 13 | | 0 22 | | 0 30 | | 0 38 | | 0 44 | | 0 50 | | 0 55 | | 0 58 | | 0 36 |
| **Liabiity & legal** | | | | | | | | | | | | | | | | | | |
| Yard | | 0 02 | | 0 03 | | 0 04 | | 0 06 | | 0 07 | | 0 08 | | 0 07 | | 0 11 | | 0 06 |
| Public | | 0 13 | | 0 22 | | 0 30 | | 0 37 | | 0 43 | | 0 49 | | 0 54 | | 0 57 | | 0 35 |
| **Admin/inspect/other** | | | | | | | | | | | | | | | | | | |
| Yard | | 0 00 | | 0 00 | | 0 00 | | 0 00 | | 0 00 | | 0 00 | | 0 00 | | 0 00 | | 0 00 |
| Public | | 0 88 | | 1 46 | | 2 00 | | 2 49 | | 2 93 | | 3 31 | | 3 63 | | 3 87 | | 2 40 |
| **Total costs** | | | | | | | | | | | | | | | | | | |
| Yard | | 101 95 | | 4 19 | | 4 77 | | 5 38 | | 6 00 | | 8 11 | | 8 51 | | 9 41 | | 17 99 |
| Public | | 52 34 | | 14 89 | | 16 75 | | 18 54 | | 20 23 | | 23 31 | | 24 66 | | 25 86 | | 23 80 |
| **Total net benefits ($/year/tree)** | | | | | | | | | | | | | | | | | | |
| Yard: West | | -97 | | 13 | | 26 | | 39 | | 52 | | 65 | | 81 | | 98 | | 35 |
| Yard: South | | -98 | | 9 | | 17 | | 27 | | 37 | | 48 | | 62 | | 79 | | 23 |
| Yard: East | | -98 | | 11 | | 22 | | 34 | | 46 | | 58 | | 74 | | 90 | | 30 |
| Public | | -48 | | 1 | | 10 | | 20 | | 31 | | 42 | | 56 | | 72 | | 24 |

# Table A3. Annual benefits, costs and net benefits at 5-year intervals and 40-year averages for a representative small broadleaf tree (dogwood, Cornus florida)

| Benefits/tree | Year 5 RU | Year 5 $ | Year 10 RU | Year 10 $ | Year 15 RU | Year 15 $ | Year 20 RU | Year 20 $ | Year 25 RU | Year 25 $ | Year 30 RU | Year 30 $ | Year 35 RU | Year 35 $ | Year 40 RU | Year 40 $ | 40-year average RU | 40-year average $ |
|---|---|---|---|---|---|---|---|---|---|---|---|---|---|---|---|---|---|---|
| **Cooling (kWh)** | | | | | | | | | | | | | | | | | | |
| Yard: West | 16 | 1 23 | 49 | 3 71 | 89 | 6 74 | 129 | 9 76 | 159 | 12 08 | 185 | 14 00 | 171 | 12 97 | 157 | 11 93 | 119 | 9 05 |
| Yard: South | 8 | 0 64 | 21 | 1 62 | 39 | 2 96 | 60 | 4 58 | 79 | 5 97 | 96 | 7 26 | 89 | 6 73 | 82 | 6 19 | 59 | 4 49 |
| Yard: East | 12 | 0 91 | 34 | 2 60 | 62 | 4 74 | 93 | 7 06 | 117 | 8 85 | 136 | 10 32 | 126 | 9 56 | 116 | 8 79 | 87 | 6 60 |
| Public | 8 | 0 62 | 19 | 1 43 | 32 | 2 42 | 46 | 3 47 | 58 | 4 38 | 69 | 5 25 | 64 | 4 86 | 59 | 4 47 | 44 | 3 36 |
| **Heating (kBtu)** | | | | | | | | | | | | | | | | | | |
| Yard: West | 71 | 0 75 | 127 | 1 32 | 182 | 1 90 | 236 | 2 46 | 275 | 2 87 | 305 | 3 19 | 282 | 2 95 | 260 | 2 71 | 217 | 2 27 |
| Yard: South | 64 | 0 67 | 83 | 0 86 | 90 | 0 94 | 97 | 1 01 | 105 | 1 10 | 117 | 1 22 | 108 | 1 13 | 100 | 1 04 | 95 | 1 00 |
| Yard: East | 56 | 0 59 | 85 | 0 89 | 117 | 1 22 | 155 | 1 62 | 185 | 1 93 | 211 | 2 21 | 196 | 2 05 | 180 | 1 88 | 148 | 1 55 |
| Public | 80 | 0 83 | 151 | 1 58 | 223 | 2 34 | 297 | 3 10 | 354 | 3 70 | 402 | 4 21 | 373 | 3 90 | 343 | 3 59 | 278 | 2 91 |
| **Net energy (kBtu)** | | | | | | | | | | | | | | | | | | |
| Yard: West | 234 | 1 98 | 615 | 5 03 | 1069 | 8 64 | 1522 | 12 23 | 1866 | 14 95 | 2150 | 17 19 | 1991 | 15 92 | 1831 | 14 64 | 1410 | 11 32 |
| Yard: South | 148 | 1 31 | 297 | 2 49 | 479 | 3 90 | 700 | 5 59 | 891 | 7 07 | 1074 | 8 49 | 995 | 7 86 | 915 | 7 23 | 687 | 5 49 |
| Yard: East | 176 | 1 50 | 428 | 3 49 | 741 | 5 96 | 1085 | 8 68 | 1350 | 10 78 | 1571 | 12 53 | 1455 | 11 60 | 1338 | 10 67 | 1018 | 8 15 |
| Public | 161 | 1 45 | 339 | 3 00 | 543 | 4 76 | 754 | 6 58 | 931 | 8 08 | 1094 | 9 46 | 1013 | 8 76 | 932 | 8 06 | 721 | 6 27 |
| **Net CO$_2$ (lb)** | | | | | | | | | | | | | | | | | | |
| Yard: West | 32 | 0 24 | 95 | 0 71 | 165 | 1 24 | 236 | 1 77 | 292 | 2 19 | 338 | 2 54 | 324 | 2 43 | 310 | 2 32 | 224 | 1 68 |
| Yard: South | 25 | 0 18 | 66 | 0 50 | 112 | 0 84 | 162 | 1 21 | 204 | 1 53 | 241 | 1 81 | 234 | 1 75 | 227 | 1 70 | 159 | 1 19 |
| Yard: East | 27 | 0 20 | 78 | 0 58 | 135 | 1 01 | 196 | 1 47 | 245 | 1 84 | 286 | 2 14 | 276 | 2 07 | 265 | 1 99 | 188 | 1 41 |
| Public | 26 | 0 20 | 72 | 0 54 | 122 | 0 91 | 173 | 1 30 | 215 | 1 61 | 252 | 1 89 | 244 | 1 83 | 236 | 1 77 | 168 | 1 26 |
| **Air pollution (lb)** | | | | | | | | | | | | | | | | | | |
| O3 uptake | 0 02 | 0 16 | 0 05 | 0 34 | 0 08 | 0 55 | 0 13 | 0 83 | 0 17 | 1 12 | 0 22 | 1 45 | 0 22 | 1 45 | 0 22 | 1 45 | 0 14 | 0 92 |
| NO2 uptake+avoided | 0 04 | 0 24 | 0 09 | 0 58 | 0 15 | 1 00 | 0 22 | 1 47 | 0 28 | 1 86 | 0 34 | 2 22 | 0 32 | 2 09 | 0 30 | 1 96 | 0 22 | 1 43 |
| SO2 uptake+avoided | 0 06 | 0 12 | 0 17 | 0 32 | 0 30 | 0 57 | 0 44 | 0 84 | 0 55 | 1 06 | 0 66 | 1 25 | 0 61 | 1 17 | 0 56 | 1 08 | 0 42 | 0 80 |
| PM10 uptake+avoided | 0 02 | 0 05 | 0 04 | 0 10 | 0 09 | 0 20 | 0 16 | 0 38 | 0 25 | 0 58 | 0 26 | 0 60 | 0 26 | 0 59 | 0 25 | 0 58 | 0 17 | 0 39 |
| VOCs avoided | 0 01 | 0 03 | 0 01 | 0 09 | 0 02 | 0 15 | 0 04 | 0 23 | 0 05 | 0 29 | 0 05 | 0 34 | 0 05 | 0 31 | 0 05 | 0 29 | 0 03 | 0 22 |
| BVOCs released | 0 00 | 0 00 | 0 00 | 0 00 | 0 00 | 0 00 | 0 00 | 0 00 | 0 00 | 0 00 | 0 00 | 0 00 | 0 00 | 0 00 | 0 00 | 0 00 | 0 00 | 0 00 |
| Avoided + net uptake | 0 15 | 0 59 | 0 36 | 1 43 | 0 65 | 2 49 | 0 99 | 3 74 | 1 31 | 4 91 | 1 53 | 5 87 | 1 46 | 5 61 | 1 38 | 5 36 | 0 98 | 3 75 |
| **Hydrology (gal)** | | | | | | | | | | | | | | | | | | |
| Rainfall interception | 160 | 1 58 | 392 | 3 88 | 691 | 6 84 | 1,098 | 10 87 | 1,545 | 15 30 | 2,077 | 20 56 | 2,077 | 20 56 | 2,077 | 20 56 | 1,265 | 12 52 |
| **Aesthetics and other benefits** | | | | | | | | | | | | | | | | | | |
| Yard | | 2 45 | | 4 09 | | 5 64 | | 6 98 | | 8 05 | | 8 84 | | 8 42 | | 7 75 | | 6 53 |
| Public | | 2 74 | | 4 57 | | 6 30 | | 7 79 | | 8 99 | | 9 87 | | 9 41 | | 8 65 | | 7 29 |
| **Total Benefits** | | | | | | | | | | | | | | | | | | |
| Yard: West | | 6 85 | | 15 14 | | 24 84 | | 35 59 | | 45 40 | | 54 99 | | 52 94 | | 50 64 | | 35 80 |
| Yard: South | | 6 12 | | 12 38 | | 19 70 | | 28 40 | | 36 85 | | 45 56 | | 44 21 | | 42 60 | | 29 48 |
| Yard: East | | 6 32 | | 13 47 | | 21 94 | | 31 75 | | 40 87 | | 49 94 | | 48 27 | | 46 34 | | 32 36 |
| Public | | 6 56 | | 13 42 | | 21 30 | | 30 28 | | 38 89 | | 47 65 | | 46 17 | | 44 41 | | 31 09 |
| **Costs ($/year/tree)** | | | | | | | | | | | | | | | | | | |
| **Tree & planting** | | | | | | | | | | | | | | | | | | |
| Yard | | 100 | | | | | | | | | | | | | | | | 12 50 |
| Public | | 44 | | | | | | | | | | | | | | | | 5 50 |
| **Pruning** | | | | | | | | | | | | | | | | | | |
| Yard | | 0 06 | | 2 78 | | 2 73 | | 2 69 | | 2 65 | | 2 61 | | 2 56 | | 2 52 | | 2 07 |
| Public | | 4 95 | | 8 93 | | 8 40 | | 7 88 | | 7 35 | | 6 83 | | 6 30 | | 5 78 | | 7 11 |
| **Remove & dispose** | | | | | | | | | | | | | | | | | | |
| Yard | | 0 64 | | 0 70 | | 1 05 | | 1 38 | | 1 71 | | 2 01 | | 2 13 | | 2 13 | | 1 38 |
| Public | | 1 06 | | 2 45 | | 3 67 | | 4 85 | | 5 97 | | 7 04 | | 7 46 | | 7 46 | | 4 70 |
| **Pest & disease** | | | | | | | | | | | | | | | | | | |
| Yard | | 0 28 | | 0 57 | | 0 84 | | 1 09 | | 1 32 | | 1 54 | | 1 60 | | 1 57 | | 1 03 |
| Public | | 0 00 | | 0 00 | | 0 00 | | 0 00 | | 0 01 | | 0 01 | | 0 01 | | 0 01 | | 0 00 |
| **Infrastructure repair** | | | | | | | | | | | | | | | | | | |
| Yard | | 0 15 | | 0 31 | | 0 47 | | 0 60 | | 0 73 | | 0 85 | | 0 89 | | 0 87 | | 0 57 |
| Public | | 1 17 | | 2 31 | | 3 27 | | 4 04 | | 4 65 | | 5 09 | | 4 98 | | 4 56 | | 3 54 |
| **Irrigation** | | | | | | | | | | | | | | | | | | |
| Yard | | 0 00 | | 0 00 | | 0 00 | | 0 00 | | 0 00 | | 0 00 | | 0 00 | | 0 00 | | 0 00 |
| Public | | 0 00 | | 0 00 | | 0 00 | | 0 00 | | 0 00 | | 0 00 | | 0 00 | | 0 00 | | 0 00 |
| **Clean-up** | | | | | | | | | | | | | | | | | | |
| Yard | | 0 02 | | 0 04 | | 0 05 | | 0 07 | | 0 08 | | 0 09 | | 0 10 | | 0 10 | | 0 06 |
| Public | | 0 13 | | 0 26 | | 0 36 | | 0 45 | | 0 52 | | 0 57 | | 0 55 | | 0 51 | | 0 39 |
| **Liability & legal** | | | | | | | | | | | | | | | | | | |
| Yard | | 0 02 | | 0 03 | | 0 05 | | 0 07 | | 0 08 | | 0 09 | | 0 10 | | 0 10 | | 0 06 |
| Public | | 0 13 | | 0 25 | | 0 36 | | 0 44 | | 0 51 | | 0 56 | | 0 54 | | 0 50 | | 0 39 |
| **Admin/inspect/other** | | | | | | | | | | | | | | | | | | |
| Yard | | 0 00 | | 0 00 | | 0 00 | | 0 00 | | 0 00 | | 0 00 | | 0 00 | | 0 00 | | 0 00 |
| Public | | 0 86 | | 1 71 | | 2 41 | | 2 99 | | 3 43 | | 3 76 | | 3 68 | | 3 37 | | 2 62 |
| **Total costs** | | | | | | | | | | | | | | | | | | |
| Yard | | 101 15 | | 4 43 | | 5 19 | | 5 91 | | 6 57 | | 7 19 | | 7 37 | | 7 29 | | 17 67 |
| Public | | 52 30 | | 15 90 | | 18 48 | | 20 65 | | 22 43 | | 23 85 | | 23 51 | | 22 17 | | 24 26 |
| **Total net benefits ($/year/tree)** | | | | | | | | | | | | | | | | | | |
| Yard: West | | -94 | | 11 | | 20 | | 30 | | 39 | | 48 | | 46 | | 43 | | 18 |
| Yard: South | | -95 | | 8 | | 15 | | 22 | | 30 | | 38 | | 37 | | 35 | | 12 |
| Yard: East | | -95 | | 9 | | 17 | | 26 | | 34 | | 43 | | 41 | | 39 | | 15 |
| Public | | -46 | | -2 | | 3 | | 10 | | 16 | | 24 | | 23 | | 22 | | 7 |

66

# Table A4. Annual benefits, costs and net benefits at 5-year intervals and 40-year averages for a representative conifer (loblolly pine, Pinus taeda)

| Benefits/tree | Year 5 RU | Year 5 $ | Year 10 RU | Year 10 $ | Year 15 RU | Year 15 $ | Year 20 RU | Year 20 $ | Year 25 RU | Year 25 $ | Year 30 RU | Year 30 $ | Year 35 RU | Year 35 $ | Year 40 RU | Year 40 $ | 40-year average RU | 40-year average $ |
|---|---|---|---|---|---|---|---|---|---|---|---|---|---|---|---|---|---|---|
| **Cooling (kWh)** | | | | | | | | | | | | | | | | | | |
| Yard: West | 25 | 1 87 | 87 | 6 58 | 147 | 11 15 | 195 | 14 83 | 237 | 17 99 | 272 | 20 68 | 309 | 23 43 | 287 | 21 82 | 195 | 14 79 |
| Yard: South | 9 | 0 70 | 36 | 2 70 | 71 | 5 35 | 108 | 8 24 | 148 | 11 26 | 186 | 14 10 | 226 | 17 18 | 243 | 18 45 | 128 | 9 75 |
| Yard: East | 15 | 1 14 | 57 | 4 35 | 105 | 7 96 | 147 | 11 17 | 184 | 13 93 | 214 | 16 27 | 244 | 18 53 | 240 | 18 24 | 151 | 11 45 |
| Public | 6 | 0 45 | 18 | 1 33 | 33 | 2 49 | 50 | 3 80 | 69 | 5 25 | 88 | 6 70 | 117 | 8 86 | 144 | 10 93 | 66 | 4 98 |
| **Heating (kBtu)** | | | | | | | | | | | | | | | | | | |
| Yard: West | 31 | 0 32 | 61 | 0 64 | 122 | 1 27 | 192 | 2 01 | 251 | 2 62 | 298 | 3 12 | 328 | 3 43 | 384 | 4 01 | 208 | 2 18 |
| Yard: South | -48 | -0 50 | -290 | -3 03 | -477 | -4 99 | -535 | -5 60 | -556 | -5 81 | -557 | -5 83 | -546 | -5 71 | -247 | -2 58 | -407 | -4 26 |
| Yard: East | -1 | -0 01 | -16 | -0 17 | 29 | 0 31 | 98 | 1 03 | 163 | 1 70 | 219 | 2 29 | 253 | 2 64 | 341 | 3 57 | 136 | 1 42 |
| Public | 58 | 0 60 | 134 | 1 40 | 224 | 2 34 | 317 | 3 32 | 403 | 4 21 | 475 | 4 97 | 527 | 5 52 | 559 | 5 85 | 337 | 3 53 |
| **Net energy (kBtu)** | | | | | | | | | | | | | | | | | | |
| Yard: West | 277 | 2 19 | 928 | 7 22 | 1591 | 12 42 | 2146 | 16 84 | 2622 | 20 62 | 3022 | 23 80 | 3415 | 26 87 | 3258 | 25 83 | 2157 | 16 97 |
| Yard: South | 44 | 0 20 | 66 | -0 33 | 228 | 0 36 | 550 | 2 64 | 928 | 5 45 | 1301 | 8 28 | 1718 | 11 48 | 2184 | 15 87 | 877 | 5 49 |
| Yard: East | 149 | 1 12 | 557 | 4 18 | 1078 | 8 27 | 1570 | 12 20 | 1999 | 15 64 | 2362 | 18 55 | 2695 | 21 18 | 2744 | 21 81 | 1644 | 12 87 |
| Public | 117 | 1 05 | 309 | 2 73 | 551 | 4 82 | 817 | 7 11 | 1094 | 9 46 | 1359 | 11 68 | 1694 | 14 37 | 2000 | 16 78 | 993 | 8 50 |
| **Net CO₂ (lb)** | | | | | | | | | | | | | | | | | | |
| Yard: West | 30 | 0 22 | 108 | 0 81 | 198 | 1 48 | 286 | 2 15 | 373 | 2 80 | 455 | 3 41 | 541 | 4 06 | 582 | 4 37 | 322 | 2 41 |
| Yard: South | 8 | 0 06 | 24 | 0 18 | 63 | 0 47 | 127 | 0 95 | 203 | 1 52 | 281 | 2 11 | 368 | 2 76 | 471 | 3 53 | 193 | 1 45 |
| Yard: East | 18 | 0 13 | 74 | 0 56 | 152 | 1 14 | 234 | 1 76 | 317 | 2 38 | 397 | 2 98 | 477 | 3 58 | 537 | 4 03 | 276 | 2 07 |
| Public | 17 | 0 13 | 58 | 0 44 | 113 | 0 85 | 178 | 1 34 | 249 | 1 87 | 320 | 2 40 | 402 | 3 01 | 482 | 3 61 | 227 | 1 71 |
| **Air pollution (lb)** | | | | | | | | | | | | | | | | | | |
| O₃ uptake | 0 04 | 0 23 | 0 09 | 0 61 | 0 18 | 1 15 | 0 28 | 1 86 | 0 42 | 2 77 | 0 58 | 3 78 | 0 77 | 5 05 | 0 99 | 6 46 | 0 42 | 2 74 |
| NO₂ uptake+avoided | 0 04 | 0 26 | 0 13 | 0 83 | 0 23 | 1 53 | 0 35 | 2 27 | 0 47 | 3 05 | 0 58 | 3 82 | 0 72 | 4 71 | 0 81 | 5 33 | 0 42 | 2 73 |
| SO₂ uptake+avoided | 0 08 | 0 15 | 0 27 | 0 52 | 0 49 | 0 93 | 0 70 | 1 33 | 0 90 | 1 72 | 1 09 | 2 08 | 1 30 | 2 48 | 1 37 | 2 61 | 0 77 | 1 48 |
| PM₁₀ uptake+avoided | 0 02 | 0 05 | 0 06 | 0 14 | 0 14 | 0 33 | 0 29 | 0 66 | 0 48 | 1 10 | 0 72 | 1 66 | 1 01 | 2 34 | 1 01 | 2 34 | 0 47 | 1 08 |
| VOCs avoided | 0 01 | 0 04 | 0 02 | 0 13 | 0 04 | 0 24 | 0 05 | 0 34 | 0 07 | 0 43 | 0 08 | 0 52 | 0 10 | 0 61 | 0 10 | 0 63 | 0 06 | 0 37 |
| BVOCs released | -0 02 | -0 13 | -0 03 | -0 20 | -0 39 | -2 44 | -1 52 | -9 49 | -3 58 | -22 32 | -6 77 | -42 18 | -11 29 | -70 32 | -11 29 | -70 32 | -4 36 | -27 18 |
| Avoided + net uptake | 0 16 | 0 60 | 0 54 | 2 03 | 0 69 | 1 74 | 0 14 | -3 03 | -1 25 | -13 24 | -3 72 | -30 32 | -7 39 | -55 12 | -7 01 | -52 95 | -2 23 | -18 79 |
| **Hydrology (gal)** | | | | | | | | | | | | | | | | | | |
| Rainfall interception | 117 | 1 16 | 431 | 4 27 | 1077 | 10 67 | 2074 | 20 53 | 3555 | 35 19 | 5315 | 52 62 | 7810 | 77 32 | 10726 | 106 19 | 3888 | 38 49 |
| **Aesthetics and other benefits** | | | | | | | | | | | | | | | | | | |
| Yard | | 0 42 | | 6 81 | | 13 33 | | 20 17 | | 27 10 | | 33 91 | | 33 12 | | 30 47 | | 20 67 |
| Public | | 0 47 | | 7 61 | | 14 89 | | 22 53 | | 30 27 | | 37 88 | | 36 99 | | 34 04 | | 23 08 |
| **Total benefits** | | | | | | | | | | | | | | | | | | |
| Yard: West | | 4 59 | | 21 14 | | 39 64 | | 56 66 | | 72 47 | | 83 42 | | 86 24 | | 113 91 | | 59 76 |
| Yard: South | | 2 43 | | 12 96 | | 26 57 | | 41 26 | | 56 03 | | 66 60 | | 69 55 | | 103 11 | | 47 31 |
| Yard: East | | 3 43 | | 17 85 | | 35 14 | | 51 63 | | 67 07 | | 77 74 | | 80 07 | | 109 55 | | 55 31 |
| Public | | 3 41 | | 17 07 | | 32 97 | | 48 48 | | 63 55 | | 74 26 | | 76 58 | | 107 67 | | 53 00 |

## Costs ($/year/tree)

| | Year 5 | | Year 10 | | Year 15 | | Year 20 | | Year 25 | | Year 30 | | Year 35 | | Year 40 | | 40-year average | |
|---|---|---|---|---|---|---|---|---|---|---|---|---|---|---|---|---|---|---|
| **Tree & planting** | | | | | | | | | | | | | | | | | | |
| Yard | 100 00 | | | | | | | | | | | | | | | | 12 50 | |
| Public | 44 00 | | | | | | | | | | | | | | | | 5 50 | |
| **Pruning** | | | | | | | | | | | | | | | | | | |
| Yard | 0 06 | | 0 06 | | 0 05 | | 0 05 | | 0 05 | | 0 05 | | 0 05 | | 0 05 | | 0 05 | |
| Public | 4 95 | | 7 48 | | 7 04 | | 6 60 | | 6 16 | | 5 72 | | 5 28 | | 4 84 | | 6 19 | |
| **Remove & dispose** | | | | | | | | | | | | | | | | | | |
| Yard | 1 79 | | 0 71 | | 1 08 | | 1 45 | | 1 82 | | 2 19 | | 2 56 | | 2 93 | | 1 56 | |
| Public | 2 99 | | 2 49 | | 3 79 | | 5 08 | | 6 37 | | 7 67 | | 8 96 | | 10 25 | | 5 26 | |
| **Pest & disease** | | | | | | | | | | | | | | | | | | |
| Yard | 0 35 | | 0 58 | | 0 87 | | 1 15 | | 1 41 | | 1 67 | | 1 92 | | 2 16 | | 1 15 | |
| Public | 0 00 | | 0 00 | | 0 00 | | 0 01 | | 0 01 | | 0 01 | | 0 01 | | 0 01 | | 0 00 | |
| **Infrastructure repair** | | | | | | | | | | | | | | | | | | |
| Yard | 0 20 | | 0 32 | | 0 48 | | 0 63 | | 0 78 | | 0 93 | | 1 06 | | 1 20 | | 0 63 | |
| Public | 1 50 | | 2 36 | | 3 37 | | 4 24 | | 4 96 | | 5 54 | | 5 98 | | 6 27 | | 3 93 | |
| **Irrigation** | | | | | | | | | | | | | | | | | | |
| Yard | 0 00 | | 0 00 | | 0 00 | | 0 00 | | 0 00 | | 0 00 | | 0 00 | | 0 00 | | 0 00 | |
| Public | 0 00 | | 0 00 | | 0 00 | | 0 00 | | 0 00 | | 0 00 | | 0 00 | | 0 00 | | 0 00 | |
| **Clean-up** | | | | | | | | | | | | | | | | | | |
| Yard | 0 02 | | 0 04 | | 0 05 | | 0 07 | | 0 09 | | 0 10 | | 0 12 | | 0 13 | | 0 07 | |
| Public | 0 17 | | 0 26 | | 0 37 | | 0 47 | | 0 55 | | 0 62 | | 0 66 | | 0 70 | | 0 44 | |
| **Liability & legal** | | | | | | | | | | | | | | | | | | |
| Yard | 0 02 | | 0 04 | | 0 05 | | 0 07 | | 0 09 | | 0 10 | | 0 12 | | 0 13 | | 0 07 | |
| Public | 0 16 | | 0 26 | | 0 37 | | 0 46 | | 0 54 | | 0 61 | | 0 65 | | 0 68 | | 0 43 | |
| **Admin/inspect/other** | | | | | | | | | | | | | | | | | | |
| Yard | 0 00 | | 0 00 | | 0 00 | | 0 00 | | 0 00 | | 0 00 | | 0 00 | | 0 00 | | 0 00 | |
| Public | 1 11 | | 0 89 | | 2 49 | | 3 13 | | 3 67 | | 4 09 | | 4 42 | | 4 63 | | 2 91 | |
| **Total costs** | | | | | | | | | | | | | | | | | | |
| Yard | 102 44 | | 1 74 | | 2 59 | | 3 42 | | 4 24 | | 5 04 | | 5 83 | | 6 60 | | 16 04 | |
| Public | 54 87 | | 13 74 | | 17 43 | | 19 98 | | 22 26 | | 24 25 | | 25 96 | | 27 38 | | 24 66 | |
| **Total net benefits** | | | | | | | | | | | | | | | | | | |
| Yard: West | -98 | | 19 | | 37 | | 53 | | 68 | | 78 | | 80 | | 107 | | 44 | |
| Yard: South | -100 | | 11 | | 24 | | 38 | | 52 | | 62 | | 64 | | 97 | | 31 | |
| Yard: East | -99 | | 16 | | 33 | | 48 | | 63 | | 73 | | 74 | | 103 | | 39 | |
| Public | -51 | | 3 | | 16 | | 28 | | 41 | | 50 | | 51 | | 80 | | 28 | |

# Appendix B: Procedures for Estimating Benefits and Costs

## Approach

### Pricing Benefits and Costs

*Public and private trees in different locations*

In this study, annual benefits and costs over a 40-year planning horizon were estimated for newly planted trees in three residential yard locations (east, south, and west of the dwelling unit) and a public streetside or park location. Trees in these hypothetical locations are called "yard" and "public" trees, respectively. Prices were assigned to each cost (e.g. planting, pruning, removal, irrigation, infrastructure repair, liability) and benefit (e.g., heating/cooling, energy savings, air-pollution reduction, stormwater-runoff reduction) through direct estimation and implied valuation of benefits as environmental externalities. This approach made it possible to estimate the net benefits of plantings in "typical" locations with "typical" tree species.

To account for differences in the mature size and growth rates of different tree species, we report results for a large (**Acer rubrum**, red maple), medium (**Magnolia grandiflora**, Southern magnolia), and small (**Cornus florida**, dogwood) broadleaf tree and for a conifer (**Pinus taeda**, loblolly pine). Results are reported for 5-year intervals for 40 years.

*Mature tree height and leaf surface area are useful indicators*

Mature tree height is frequently used to characterize large, medium, and small species because matching tree height to available overhead space is an important design consideration. However, in this analysis, leaf surface area (LSA) and crown diameter were also used to characterize **mature tree size**. These additional measurements are useful indicators for many functional benefits of trees that relate to leaf–atmosphere processes (e.g., interception, transpiration, photosynthesis). Tree growth rates, dimensions, and LSA estimates are based on tree growth modeling.

### Growth Modeling

Growth models are based on data collected in Charlotte, NC. An inventory of Charlotte's street trees was provided by the City Engineering Landscape Management staff. The inventory was conducted from 2002 through 2004 and included 85,146 trees representing 215 species.

Tree-growth models developed from Charlotte data were used as the basis for modeling tree growth for this report. Using Charlotte's tree inventory, a stratified random sample of 21 tree species was measured to establish relations between tree age, size, leaf area and biomass.

For the growth models, information spanning the life cycle of predominant tree species was collected. The inventory was stratified into the following nine diameter-at-breast-height (DBH) classes:

- 0–3 in (0–7.6 cm)
- 3–6 in (7.6–15.2 cm)
- 6–12 in (15.2–30.5 cm)
- 12–18 in (30.5–45.7 cm)
- 18–24 in (45.7–61.0 cm)
- 24–30 in (61.0–76.2 cm)
- 30–36 in (76.2–91.4 cm)
- 36–42 in (91.4–106.7 cm)
- >42 in (106.7 cm)

Thirty to fifty trees of each species were randomly selected for surveying, along with an equal number of alternative trees. Tree measurements included DBH (to nearest 0.1 cm by sonar measuring device), tree crown and bole height (to nearest 0.5 m by clinometer), crown diameter in two directions (parallel and perpendicular to nearest street to nearest 0.5 m by sonar measuring device), tree condition and location. Replacement trees were sampled when trees from the original sample population could not be located. Tree age was determined by street-tree managers. Fieldwork was conducted in August 2004.

Crown volume and leaf area were estimated from computer processing of tree-crown images obtained using a digital camera. The method has shown greater accuracy than other techniques (±20% of actual leaf area) in estimating crown volume and leaf area of open-grown trees (Peper and McPherson 2003).

Linear regression was used to fit predictive models with DBH as a function of age for each of the 21 sampled species. Predictions of leaf surface area (LSA), crown diameter, and height metrics were modeled as a function of DBH using best-fit models. After inspecting the growth curves for each species, we selected the typical large, medium, and small tree species for this report.

### Reporting Results

Results are reported in terms of annual values per tree planted. However, to make these calculations realistic, mortality rates are included. Based on our survey of regional municipal foresters and commercial arborists, this analysis assumed that 45% of the hypothetical planted

*Annual values reported*

trees died over the 40-year period. Annual mortality rates were 2% for the first 5 years, and 1% per year after that, or 45% total. This accounting approach "grows" trees in different locations and uses computer simulation to directly calculate the annual flow of benefits and costs as trees mature and die (McPherson 1992).

*Benefits and costs are connected with size of tree*

Benefits and costs are directly connected with tree-size variables such as trunk DBH, tree canopy cover, and LSA. For instance, pruning and removal costs usually increase with tree size, expressed as DBH. For some parameters, such as sidewalk repair, costs are negligible for young trees but increase relatively rapidly as tree roots grow large enough to heave pavement. For other parameters, such as air-pollutant uptake and rainfall interception, benefits are related to tree canopy cover and leaf area.

*Annual vs. periodic costs*

Most benefits occur on an annual basis, but some costs are periodic. For instance, street trees may be pruned on regular cycles but are removed in a less regular fashion (e.g., when they pose a hazard or soon after they die). In this analysis, most costs and benefits are reported for the year in which they occur. However, periodic costs such as pruning, pest and disease control, and infrastructure repair are presented on an average annual basis. Although spreading one-time costs over each year of a maintenance cycle does not alter the 40-year nominal expenditure, it can lead to inaccuracies if future costs are discounted to the present.

### *Benefit and Cost Valuation*

#### *Source of cost estimates*

*Source of cost estimates*

Frequency and costs of tree management were estimated based on surveys with municipal foresters from Charlotte, NC, Richmond, VA, Cumming, GA, Columbus, GA, and Chattanooga, TN. In addition, commercial arborists in Charlotte, NC, and Roswell, GA, provided information on tree management costs on residential properties.

#### *Pricing benefits*

*Pricing benefits*

Electricity and natural-gas prices for utilities serving Charlotte were used to quantify energy savings for the region. **Control costs** were used to estimate willingness to pay for air quality improvements. For example, the prices for air-quality benefits were estimated using marginal control costs (Wang and Santini 1995). If a developer is willing to pay an average of $1 per pound of treated and controlled pollutant to meet minimum standards, then the air pollution mitigation value of a tree that intercepts one pound of pollution, eliminating the need for control, should be $1.

# Calculating Benefits

## Calculating Energy Benefits

The prototypical building used as a basis for the simulations was typical of post-1980 construction practices, and represents approximately one-third of the total single-family residential housing stock in the Piedmont region. The house was a one-story, wood-frame, slab-on-grade building with a conditioned floor area of 2,180 ft$^2$ (203 m$^2$), window area (double-glazed) of 242 ft$^2$ (22.5 m$^2$), and wall, ceiling and foundation insulation of R11, R27, and R19, respectively. The central cooling system had a **seasonal energy efficiency ratio (SEER)** of 10, and the natural-gas furnace had an **annual fuel utilization efficiency (AFUE)** of 78%. Building footprints were square, reflecting average impacts for a large number of buildings (McPherson and Simpson 1999). Buildings were simulated with 1.5-ft (0.45-m) overhangs. Blinds had a visual density of 37% and were assumed to be closed when the air conditioner was operating. Summer thermostat settings were 78°F (25°C); winter settings were 68°F (20°C) during the day and 60°F (16°C) at night. Because the prototype building was larger, but more energy efficient, than most other construction types, our projected energy savings can be considered similar to those for older, less thermally efficient, but smaller buildings. The energy simulations relied on typical meteorological data from Charlotte (Marion and Urban 1995).

*Using a typical single family residence for energy simulations*

### Calculating energy savings

The dollar value of energy savings was based on regional average residential electricity and natural-gas prices of $0.076/**kWh** and $1.046/**therm**, respectively. Electricity and natural-gas prices were for 2005 for North Carolina (Duke Power 2005 and Piedmont Natural Gas 2004, respectively). Homes were assumed to have central air conditioning and natural-gas heating.

### Calculating shade effects

Residential yard trees were within 60 ft (18 m) of homes so as to directly shade walls and windows. Shade effects of these trees on building energy use were simulated for large, medium, and small trees at three tree-to-building distances, following methods outlined by McPherson and Simpson (1999). The large tree (red maple) had a visual density of 74% during summer and 30% during winter. The medium tree (magnolia) had a density of 21% during summer and winter, the small tree (dogwood) had densities of 70% during summer and 25% during winter, and the conifer (loblolly pine) had a density of 28% year round. Leaf-off values for use in calculating winter shade were based on published values where available (McPherson 1984;

Hammond et al. 1980). Foliation periods for deciduous trees were obtained from the literature (McPherson 1984; Hammond et al.1980) and adjusted for Charlotte's climate based on consultation with forestry supervisors (Hartel 2005).

Large trees were leafless November 25–May 14, medium trees and conifers were evergreen, and small trees were leafless October 20–April 29. Results of shade effects for each tree were averaged over distance and weighted by occurrence within each of three distance classes: 28% at 10–20 ft (3–6 m), 68% at 20–40 ft (6–12 m), and 4% at 40–60 ft (12–18 m) (McPherson and Simpson 1999). Results are reported for trees shading east-, south-, and west-facing surfaces. Our results for public trees are conservative in that we assumed that they do not provide shading benefits. For example, in Modesto, CA 15% of total annual dollar energy savings from street trees was due to shade and 85% due to **climate effects** (McPherson et al. 1999a).

### Calculating climate effects

In addition to localized shade effects, which were assumed to accrue only to residential yard trees, lowered air temperatures and wind speeds from increased neighborhood tree cover (referred to as climate effects) produced a net decrease in demand for winter heating and summer cooling (reduced wind speeds by themselves may increase or decrease cooling demand, depending on the circumstances). Climate effects on energy use, air temperature and wind speed, as a function of neighborhood canopy cover, were estimated from published values (McPherson and Simpson 1999). Climate effects were estimated by simulating effects of wind and air-temperature reductions on energy use. Climate effects accrued for both public and yard trees.

### Calculating windbreak effects

Trees near buildings result in additional wind-speed reductions beyond those from the aggregate effects of neighborhood trees. This leads to a small additional reduction in annual heating energy use of about 0.4% per tree for the Piedmont region (McPherson and Simpson 1999). Yard and public conifer trees were assumed to be windbreaks, and therefore located where they did not increase heating loads by obstructing winter sun. Windbreak effects were not attributed to broadleaf trees, since their crowns are leafless and above the ground, and therefore do not block winds near ground level.

## Atmospheric Carbon Dioxide Reduction

### Calculating reduction in $CO_2$ emissions from power plants

Conserving energy in buildings can reduce $CO_2$ emissions from power plants. These avoided emissions were calculated as the product of energy savings for heating and cooling based on the $CO_2$ **emission factors** (**Table B1**) and were based on data for North Carolina where the average fuel mix is 0.29% hydro, 0.3% natural gas, 43.1% coal, and 56.2% nuclear (US EPA 2003). The value of $15/ton $CO_2$ reduction (**Table B1**) was based on the average of high and low estimates by CO2e.com (2005).

## Calculating carbon storage

Sequestration, the net rate of $CO_2$ storage in above- and belowground biomass over the course of one growing season, was calculated using tree height and DBH data with biomass equations (Pillsbury et al. 1998). Volume estimates were converted to green and dry-weight estimates (Markwardt 1930) and divided by 78% to incorporate root biomass. Dry-weight biomass was converted to carbon (50%) and these values were converted to $CO_2$. The amount of $CO_2$ sequestered each year is the annual increment of $CO_2$ stored as trees increase their biomass.

## Calculating $CO_2$ released by power equipment

**Tree-related emissions** of $CO_2$, based on gasoline and diesel fuel consumption during tree care in our survey cities, were calculated using the value 0.739 lb $CO_2$/in DBH (0.132 kg $CO_2$ per cm DBH). This amount may overestimate $CO_2$ release associated with less intensively maintained residential yard trees.

## Calculating $CO_2$ released during decomposition

To calculate $CO_2$ released through decomposition of dead woody biomass, we conservatively estimated that dead trees were removed and mulched in the year that death occurred, and that 80% of their stored carbon was released to the atmosphere as $CO_2$ in the same year (McPherson and Simpson 1999).

## Air Quality Impacts

### Calculating reduction in air pollutant emissions

Reductions in building energy use also result in reduced emission of air pollutants from power plants and space-heating equipment. Volatile organic hydrocarbons (VOCs) and nitrogen dioxide ($NO_2$)—both precursors of ozone formation—as well as sulfur dioxide ($SO_2$) and particulate matter of <10 micron diameter ($PM_{10}$) were considered. Changes in average annual emissions and their monetary values were calculated in the same way as for $CO_2$, using utility-specific emissions factors for electricity and heating fuels (Ottinger et al. 1990; US EPA 1998). The price of emissions savings were derived from models that calculate the marginal cost of controlling different pollutants to meet

**Table B1. Emissions factors and implied value of benefits for $CO_2$ and critical air pollutants**

| | Emission Factor | | |
| | Electricity (lb/MWh)[a] | Natural gas (lb/MBtu)[b] | Implied value ($/lb)[c] |
|---|---|---|---|
| $CO_2$ | 845 | 118 | 0.0075 |
| $NO_2$ | 1.981 | 0.1020 | 6.55 |
| $SO_2$ | 5.113 | 0.0006 | 1.91 |
| $PM_{10}$ | 0.434 | 0.0075 | 2.31 |
| VOCs | 0.433 | 0.0054 | 6.23 |

[a]US EPA 2003, except Ottinger et al. 1990 for VOCs
[b]US EPA 1998
[c]$CO_2$ from CO2e.com (2005). Value for others based on the methods of Wang and Santini (1995) using emissions concentrations from US EPA (2003) and population estimates from the US Census Bureau (2002)

air quality standards (Wang and Santini 1995). Emissions concentrations were obtained from US EPA (2003; **Table B1**), and population estimates from the US Census Bureau (2002).

*Calculating pollutant uptake by trees*

Trees also remove pollutants from the atmosphere. The modeling method we applied was developed by Scott et al. (1998). It calculates **hourly pollutant dry deposition** per tree expressed as the product of deposition velocity ($Vd =1/[Ra + Rb + Rc]$), pollutant concentration (C), canopy-projection area (CP), and a time step, where $Ra$, $Rb$ and $Rc$ are aerodynamic, boundary layer, and stomatal resistances. Hourly deposition velocities for each pollutant were calculated during the growing season using estimates for the resistances ($Ra + Rb + Rc$) for each hour throughout the year. Hourly concentrations for $NO_2$, $SO_2$, $O_3$ and $PM_{10}$ and hourly meteorological data (i.e., air temperature, wind speed, solar radiation) from Charlotte and the surrounding area for 2003 were obtained from the North Carolina Department of Environment and Natural Resources. The year 2003 was chosen because data were available and it closely approximated long-term, regional climate records. To set a value for pollutant uptake by trees we used the procedure described above for emissions reductions (**Table B1**). The monetary value for $NO_2$ was used for ozone.

*Estimating BVOC emissions from trees*

Annual emissions for biogenic volatile organic compounds (BVOCs) were estimated for the three tree species using the algorithms of Guenther et al. (1991, 1993). Annual emissions were simulated during the growing season over 40 years. The emission of carbon as isoprene was expressed as a product of the base emission rate (µg C/g dry foliar biomass/hr), adjusted for sunlight and temperature and the amount of dry, foliar biomass present in the tree. Monoterpene emissions were estimated using a base emission rate adjusted for temperature. The base emission rates for the three species were based on values reported in the literature (Benjamin and Winer 1998). Hourly emissions were summed to get monthly and annual emissions.

Annual dry foliar biomass was derived from field data collected in Charlotte, NC, during the summer of 2004. The amount of foliar biomass present for each year of the simulated tree's life was unique for each species. Hourly air temperature and solar radiation data for 2003 described in the pollutant uptake section were used as model inputs.

*Calculating net air-quality benefits*

Net air-quality benefits were calculated by subtracting the costs associated with BVOC emissions from benefits due to pollutant uptake and avoided power plant emissions. The ozone-reduction benefit from lowering summertime air temperatures, thereby reducing hydrocarbon emissions from **anthropogenic** and biogenic sources were estimated as a function of canopy cover following McPherson and Simpson (1999). They used peak summer air temperatures reductions of 0.4°F for each percentage increase in canopy cover. Hourly changes in air temperature were calculated by reducing this peak air temperature at every hour based on hourly maximum and minimum temperature for that day, and the maximum and minimum values of total global solar radiation for the year. Simulation results from Los Angeles indicate that ozone reduction benefits of planting with "low-emitting" species exceeded costs associated with their BVOC emissions (Taha 1996).

### Stormwater Benefits

#### Estimating rainfall interception by tree canopies

A numerical simulation model was used to estimate annual rainfall interception (Xiao et al. 2000). The interception model accounted for water intercepted by the tree, as well as throughfall and **stem flow**. Intercepted water is stored temporarily on canopy leaf and bark surfaces. Rainwater drips from leaf surfaces and flows down the stem surface to the ground or evaporates. Tree-canopy parameters that affect interception include species, leaf and stem surface areas, **shade coefficient**s (visual density of the crown), foliation periods, and tree dimensions (e.g., tree height, crown height, crown diameter, and DBH). Tree-height data were used to estimate wind speed at different heights above the ground and resulting rates of evaporation.

The volume of water stored in the tree crown was calculated from crown-projection area (area under tree dripline), leaf area indices (LAI, the ratio of leaf surface area to crown projection area), and the depth of water captured by the canopy surface. Gap fractions, foliation periods, and tree surface saturation storage capacity influence the amount of projected throughfall. Tree surface saturation was 0.04 inches for all trees. Hourly meteorological and rainfall data for 2004 from the Douglas International Airport, NC (KCLT) (Station: KCLT – Douglas International Airport, Charlotte, NC; latitude 35.21° N, longitude -80.94° W) were used for this simulation. Annual precipitation during 2004 was 56.2 in (1,426 mm). Storm events less than 0.2 in (5 mm) were assumed not to produce runoff and were dropped from the analysis. More complete descriptions of the interception model can be found in Xiao et al. (1998, 2000).

#### Calculating water quality protection and flood control benefit

Treatment of runoff is one way of complying with federal Clean Water Act regulations by preventing contaminated stormwater from entering local waterways. Stormwater management fees for Charlotte, NC, were used as the basis for calculating the implied value of each gallon of stormwater intercepted by trees. In Charlotte, monthly stormwater fees are assessed to cover the cost of its stormwater management program. These fees are used as a proxy for the public's willingness to pay for stormwater management. Residential and commercial customers are charged the same amount, $93 per acre of impervious surface per month. The cost of controlling runoff from a 10-year storm is used as the basis for valuing rainfall interception by trees in Charlotte. This event is selected because most Best Management Practices (BMPs), such as retention-detention basins, are designed to operate effectively for storm events up to this size. Runoff from larger events are assumed to bypass BMPs, directly entering the system without pretreatment. Also, tree crown interception does not increase after crowns are saturated, which usually occurs before storm events reach this magnitude. Runoff from 1 acre of impervious surface for a 10-year, 24-hour storm event (4.9 in) is 113,114 gal, assuming an average runoff coefficient of 0.85. Assuming an annual stormwater management fee of $1,116 per acre of impervious surface, the resulting control cost is $0.0099 per gal.

## Aesthetic and Other Benefits

Many benefits attributed to urban trees are difficult to translate into economic terms. Beautification, privacy, wildlife habitat, shade that increases human comfort, sense of place and well-being are services that are difficult to price. However, the value of some of these benefits may be captured in the property values of the land on which trees stand.

To estimate the value of these "other" benefits, we applied results of research that compared differences in sales prices of houses to statistically quantify the difference associated with trees. All else being equal, the difference in sales price reflects the willingness of buyers to pay for the benefits and costs associated with trees. This approach has the virtue of capturing in the sales price both the benefits and costs of trees as perceived by the buyers. Limitations to this approach include difficulty determining the value of individual trees on a property, the need to extrapolate results from studies done years ago in the East and South to the Midwest region, and the need to extrapolate results from front-yard trees on residential properties to trees in other locations (e.g., back yards, streets, parks, and non-residential land).

### A large tree adds value to a home

Anderson and Cordell (1988) surveyed 844 single-family residences in Athens, Georgia and found that each large front-yard tree was associated with a 0.88% increase in the average home sales price. This percentage of sales price was utilized as an indicator of the additional value a resident in the Midwest region would gain from selling a home with a large tree.

The sales price of residential properties varied widely by location within the region; for example, in 2004 median home prices ranged from \$121,000 in Jackson, MS, to \$362,000 in Washington, DC. By averaging the values for seven cities we calculated the average home price for Piedmont communities as \$164,200. Therefore, the value of a large tree that added 0.88% to the sales price of such a home was \$1,445. In order to estimate annual benefits, the total added value was divided by the leaf surface area of a 30-year-old willow oak (\$1,445/7,374 ft$^2$) to yield the base value of LSA, \$0.19/ft$^2$. This value was multiplied by the amount of leaf surface area added to the tree during one year of growth.

## Calculating the aesthetic value of residential yard trees

To calculate the base value for a large tree on private residential property we assumed that a 30-year-old willow oak in the front yard increased the property sales price by \$1,445. Approximately 75% of all yard trees, however, are in backyards (Richards et al. 1984). Lacking specific research findings, it was assumed that backyard trees had 75% of the impact on "curb appeal" and sales price compared to front-yard trees. The average annual aesthetic benefit for a tree on private property was estimated as \$0.15/ft$^2$ (\$1.60/m$^2$) LSA. To estimate annual benefits, this value was multiplied by the amount of leaf surface area added to the tree during one year of growth.

## Calculating the base value of a street tree

The base value of street trees was calculated in the same way as front yard trees. However, because street trees may be adjacent to land with little value or resale potential, an adjusted value was calculated. An analysis of street trees in Modesto, CA, sampled from aerial photographs (sample size 8%), found that 15% were located adjacent to nonresidential or commercial property (McPherson et al. 1999b). We assumed that 33% of these trees—or 5% of the entire street-tree population—produced no benefits associated with property value increases.

Although the impact of parks on real estate values has been reported (Hammer et al. 1974; Schroeder 1982; Tyrvainen 1999), to our knowledge the on-site and external benefits of park trees alone have not been isolated (More et al. 1988). After reviewing the literature and recognizing an absence of data, we made the conservative estimate that park trees had half the impact on property prices as street trees. Additionally, not all street trees are as effective as front-yard trees in increasing property values. For example, trees adjacent to multifamily housing units will not increase the property value at the same rate as trees in front of single-family homes. Therefore, a citywide street tree reduction factor (0.923) was applied to prorate trees' value based on the assumption that trees adjacent to different land-uses make different contributions to property sales prices. For this analysis, the street reduction factor reflects the distribution of street trees in Charlotte by land-use. Reduction factors were single-home residential (100%), multi-home residential (70%), small commercial (66%), industrial/in-stititutional/large commercial (40%), park/vacant/other (40%) (Gonzales 2004, McPherson 2001).

Given these assumptions, typical large street and park trees we estimated to increase property values by \$0.18 and \$0.10/ft$^2$ (\$1.97 and \$1.06/m$^2$) LSA, respectively. Assuming that 80% of all municipal trees were on streets and 20% in parks, a weighted average benefit of \$0.166/ft$^2$ (\$1.78/m$^2$) LSA was calculated for each tree.

## *Calculating Costs*

Tree management costs were estimated based on surveys with municipal foresters from Chattanooga, TN, Columbus, GA, Cumming, GA, Richmond, VA, and Charlotte, NC. In addition, commercial arborists in Roswell, GA and Charlotte, NC, provided information on tree management costs on residential properties.

### *Planting*

Planting costs include the cost of the tree and the cost for planting, staking, and mulching the tree. Based on our survey of Piedmont municipal and commercial arborists, planting costs depend on tree size. Costs ranged from \$200 for a 1-in tree to \$825 for a 3-in tree. In this analysis we assumed that a 3-in yard tree was planted at a cost of \$500. The cost for planting a 2.5-in public tree was \$220.

### *Pruning*

#### *Pruning costs for public trees*

After studying data from municipal forestry programs and their contractors, we assumed that young public trees were inspected and pruned once during the first 5 years after planting, at a cost of \$22 per tree. After this training period, pruning occurred once every 5 years for small trees (<20 ft tall) at a cost of \$44 per tree. Medium trees (20–40 ft tall) were inspected/pruned every 10 years, and large trees (>40 ft tall) every 15 years. More expensive equipment and more time was required to prune medium (\$105 per tree) and large trees (\$191 per tree) than small trees. Conifers require much less substantial pruning, usually only raising of lower branches which can be accomplished from the ground. The price was set, therefore, equal to that of training ($22 per tree). After factoring in pruning frequency, annualized costs were $5, $22, $26, and $38 per tree for public young, and small, medium, and large mature broadleaf trees, respectively, and $5 per tree for conifers.

### Pruning costs for yard trees

Based on findings from our survey of commercial arborists in the Piedmont region, pruning cycles for yard trees were similar to public trees, but only 20% of all private trees were professionally pruned (**contract rate**). However, the number of professionally pruned trees grows as the trees grow. We assumed that professionals are paid to prune all large trees, 60% of the medium trees, and only 6% of the small and young trees and conifers (Summit and McPherson 1998). Using these contract rates, along with average pruning prices ($20, $25, $250, and $350 for young, small, medium, and large trees, respectively), the average annual costs for pruning a yard tree were $0.06, $0.06, $3.00, and $4.69 for young, small, medium, and large trees. Pruning of private conifers was calculated as above for public trees and valued as $0.06 per tree per year.

## Tree and Stump Removal

The costs for tree removal and disposal were $28 per inch ($10.92 per cm) DBH for public trees, and $85 per inch ($33.15 per cm) DBH for yard trees. Stump removal costs were $6 per inch ($2.34 per cm) DBH for public and $137 per inch ($53.43 per cm) DBH for yard trees. Therefore, total costs for removal and disposal of trees and stumps were $35 per inch ($13.65 per cm) DBH for public trees, and $222 per inch ($86.58 per cm) DBH for yard trees.

## Pest and Disease Control

Pest and disease control measures in the Piedmont are minimal. Expenditures averaged about $0.01 per tree per year or approximately $0.0005 per inch ($0.000195 per cm) DBH for public trees. Results of our survey indicated that only 20% of all yard trees were treated, and the amount of money spent averaged $96 per tree. The estimated cost for treating pests and diseases in yard trees was $19.82 per tree per year or $1.80 per inch ($0.70 per cm) DBH.

## Irrigation Costs

Rain falls fairly regularly (3–4 in/month) throughout most of the Piedmont region and sufficiently that irrigation is not usually needed. Only one of seven municipalities surveyed provides irrigation to street trees. Therefore, we did not include any costs for this category.

## Other Costs for Public and Yard Trees

Other costs associated with the management of trees include expenditures for infrastructure repair/root pruning, leaf-litter clean-up, litigation/liability, and inspection/administration. Cost data were obtained from the municipal arborist survey and assume that 50% of public trees are street trees and 50% are park trees. Costs for park trees tend to be lower than for street trees because there are fewer conflicts with infrastructure such as power lines and sidewalks.

### Infrastructure conflict costs

Many Piedmont municipalities have a substantial number of large, old trees and deteriorating sidewalks. As trees and sidewalks age, roots can cause damage to sidewalks, curbs, paving, and sewer lines. Sidewalk repair is typically one of the largest expenses for public trees (McPherson and Peper 1995). Infrastructure-related expenditures for public trees in Piedmont communities were high relative to other regions, averaging approximately $6.40 per tree on an annual basis. Roots from most trees in residential yards do not damage sidewalks and sewers. Therefore, the cost for yard trees was estimated to be only 2% of the cost for public trees.

### Liability costs

Urban trees can incur costly payments and legal fees due to trip-and-fall claims. A survey of western U.S. cities showed that an average of 8.8% of total tree-related expenditures was spent on tree-related liability (McPherson 2000). Our survey found that Piedmont communities spend $0.58 per tree per year on average ($0.0105/in DBH). Because street trees are in closer proximity to sidewalks and sewer lines than most trees on yard property, we assumed that legal costs for yard trees were 10% of those for public trees (McPherson et al. 1993).

### Litter and storm clean-up costs

The average annual per tree cost for litter clean-up (i.e., street sweeping, storm-damage clean-up) was $0.59 per tree ($0.0107/in [$0.0041 per cm] DBH). This value was based on average annual litter clean-up costs and storm clean-up, assuming a large storm results in extraordinary costs about once a decade. Because most residential yard trees are not littering the streets with leaves, it was assumed that clean-up costs for yard trees were 10% of those for public trees.

### Green-waste disposal costs

Green-waste disposal and recycling costs were negligible for our survey of Piedmont communities because 95–100% of green waste is recycled as mulch, compost, firewood, or other products. Fees from the sale of these products largely offset the costs of processing and hauling. Arborists and residents pay tipping fees for disposal of green waste, but these disposal costs are already included in the pruning and removal estimates.

### Inspection and administration costs

Municipal tree programs have administrative costs for salaries of supervisors and clerical staff, operating costs, and overhead. Our survey found that the average annual cost for inspection and administration associated with street- and park-tree management was $3.14 per tree ($0.29/in DBH). Trees on private property do not accrue this expense.

## Calculating Net Benefits

### Benefits Accrue at Different Scales

When calculating net benefits, it is important to recognize that trees produce benefits that accrue both on- and off-site. Benefits are realized at four different scales: parcel, neighborhood, community, and global. For example, property owners with on-site trees not only benefit from increased property values, but they may also directly benefit from improved human health (e.g., reduced exposure to cancer-causing UV radiation) and greater psychological well-being through visual and direct contact with plants. However, on the cost side, increased health care may be incurred because of nearby trees due to allergies and respiratory ailments related to pollen. We assumed that these intangible benefits and costs were reflected in what we term "aesthetics and other benefits."

The property owner can obtain additional economic benefits from on-site trees depending on their location and condition. For example, carefully located on-site trees can provide air-conditioning savings by shading windows and walls and cooling building microclimates. This benefit can extend to adjacent neighbors who benefit from shade and air-temperature reductions that lower their cooling costs.

Neighborhood attractiveness and property values can be influenced by the extent of tree canopy cover on individual properties. At the community scale, benefits are realized through cleaner air and water, as well as social, educational, and employment and job training benefits that can reduce costs for health care, welfare, crime prevention, and other social service programs.

Reductions in atmospheric $CO_2$ concentrations due to trees are an example of benefits that are realized at the global scale.

*The sum of all benefits is…*

Annual benefits are calculated as:

$$B = E + AQ + CO_2 + H + A$$

where

$E$ = value of net annual energy savings (cooling and heating)

$AQ$ = value of annual air-quality improvement (pollutant uptake, avoided power plant emissions, and BVOC emissions)

$CO_2$ = value of annual carbon dioxide reductions (sequestration, avoided emissions, release due to tree care and decomposition)

$H$ = value of annual stormwater-runoff reductions

$A$ = value of annual aesthetics and other benefits

On the other side of the benefit–cost equation are costs for tree planting and management. Expenditures are borne by property owners (irrigation, pruning, and removal) and the community (pollen and other health care costs). Annual costs ($C$) are the sum of residential yard tree costs ($C_Y$) and public tree costs ($C_P$) where:

*The sum of all costs is…*

$$C_Y = P + T + R + D + I + S + Cl + L$$
$$C_P = P + T + R + D + I + S + Cl + L + A$$

where

$P$ = cost of tree and planting

$T$ = average annual tree pruning cost

$R$ = annualized tree and stump removal and disposal cost

$D$ = average annual pest- and disease-control cost

$I$ = annual irrigation cost

$S$ = average annual cost to repair/mitigate infrastructure damage

$Cl$ = annual litter and storm clean-up cost

$L$ = average annual cost for litigation and settlements due to tree-related claims

$A$ = annual program administration, inspection, and other costs

Net benefits are calculated as the difference between total benefits and costs:

*Net benefits are…*

Net benefits = $B - C$

Benefit–cost ratios (BCR) are calculated as the ratio of benefits to costs:

BCR = $B / C$

## *Limitations of this Study*

This analysis does not account for the wide variety of trees planted in the Piedmont communities or their diverse placement. It does not incorporate the full range of climatic differences within the region that influence potential energy, air-quality, and hydrology benefits. Estimating aesthetics and other benefits is difficult because the science in this area is not well developed. We considered only residential and municipal tree cost scenarios, but realize that the costs associated with planting and managing trees can vary widely depending on program characteristics. For example, our analysis does not incorporate costs incurred by utility companies and passed on to customers for maintenance of trees under power lines. However, as described by examples in Chapter 3, local cost data can be substituted for the data in this report to evaluate the benefits and costs of alternative programs.

*More research is needed*

In this analysis, results are presented in terms of future values of benefits and costs, not present values. Thus, findings do not incorporate the time value of money or inflation. We assume that the user intends to invest in community forests and our objective is to identify the relative magnitudes of future costs and benefits. If the user is interested in comparing an investment in urban forestry with other investment opportunities, it is important to discount all future benefits and costs to the beginning of the investment period. For example, trees with a future value of $100,000 in 10 years have a present value of $55,840, assuming a 6% annual interest rate.

*Future benefits are not discounted to present value*

# Glossary of Terms

**Annual fuel utilization efficiency (AFUE)**: A measure of space heating equipment efficiency defined as the fraction of energy output/energy input.

**Anthropogenic**: Produced by humans.

**Avoided power plant emissions**: Reduced emissions of $CO_2$ or other pollutants that result from reductions in building energy use due to the moderating effect of trees on climate. Reduced energy use for heating and cooling results in reduced demand for electrical energy, which translates into fewer emissions by power plants.

**Biodiversity**: The variety of life forms in a given area. Diversity can be categorized in terms of the number of species, the variety in the area's plant and animal communities, the genetic variability of the animals or plants, or a combination of these elements.

**Biogenic**: Produced by living organisms.

**Biogenic volatile organic compounds (BVOCs)**: Hydrocarbon compounds from vegetation (e.g., isoprene, monoterpene) that exist in the ambient air and contribute to the formation of smog and/or may themselves be toxic. Emission rates (ug/g/hr) used for this report follow Benjamin and Winer (1998):

> **Acer rubrum**: 0.0 (isoprene); 2.8 (monoterpene)
> **Magnolia grandiflora**: 0.0 (isoprene); 5.9 (monoterpene)
> **Cornus florida**: 0.0 (isoprene); 0.0 (monoterpene)
> **Pinus taeda**: 0.0 (isoprene); 5.1 (monoterpene)

**Canopy**: A layer or multiple layers of branches and foliage at the top or crown of a forest's trees.

**Canopy Cover**: The area of land surface that is covered by tree canopy, as seen from above.

**Climate**: The average weather for a particular region and time period (usually 30 years). Weather describes the short-term state of the atmosphere; climate is the average pattern of weather for a particular region. Climatic elements include precipitation, temperature, humidity, sunshine, wind velocity, phenomena such as fog, frost, and hail storms, and other measures of weather.

**Climate effects**: Impact on residential energy use (kg $CO_2$ per tree per year) from trees located more than 50 ft (15 m) from a building due to reductions in wind speeds and summer air temperatures.

**Community forests**: The sum of all woody and associated vegetation in and around human settlements, ranging from small rural villages to metropolitan regions.

**Conifer**: A tree that bears cones and has needle-like leaves.

**Contract rate**: The percentage of residential trees cared for by commercial arborists; the proportion of trees contracted out for a specific service (e.g., pruning or pest management).

**Control costs**: The marginal cost of reducing air pollutants using best available control technologies.

**Crown**: The branches and foliage at the top of a tree.

**Cultivar**: Derived from "cultivated variety." Denotes certain cultivated plants that are clearly distinguishable from others by any characteristic, and that when reproduced (sexually or asexually), retain their distinguishing characteristics. In the United States, variety is often considered synonymous with cultivar.

**Deciduous**: Trees or shrubs that lose their leaves every fall.

**Diameter at breast height** (DBH): The diameter of a tree outside the bark measured 4.5 feet (1.37 m) above the ground on the uphill side (where applicable) of the tree.

**Emission factor**: The rate of $CO_2$, $NO_2$, $SO_2$, and $PM_{10}$ output resulting from the consumption of electricity, natural gas or any other fuel source.

**Evapotranspiration (ET)**: The total loss of water by evaporation from the soil surface and by transpiration from plants, from a given area, and during a specified period of time.

**Evergreens**: Trees or shrubs that are never entirely leafless. Evergreens may be broadleaved or coniferous (cone-bearing with needle-like leaves).

**Greenspace**: Urban trees, forests, and associated vegetation in and around human settlements, ranging from small communities in rural settings to metropolitan regions.

**Hardscape**: Paving and other impervious ground surfaces that reduce infiltration of water into the soil.

**Heat sink**: Paving, buildings, and other built surfaces that store heat energy from the sun.

**Hourly pollutant dry deposition**: Removal of gases from the atmosphere by direct transfer to natural surfaces and absorption of gases and particles by natural surfaces such as vegetation, soil, water or snow.

**Interception**: Amount of rainfall held on tree leaves and stem surfaces.

**kBtu**: A unit of heat, measured as 1,000 British thermal units. One kBtu is equivalent to 0.293 kWh.

**kWh (kilowatt-hour)**: A unit of work or energy, measured as one kilowatt (1,000 watts) of power expended for one hour. One kWh is equivalent to 3.412 kBtu.

**Leaf surface area (LSA)**: Measurement of area of one side of a leaf or leaves.

**Mature tree**: A tree that has reached a desired size or age for its intended use. Size, age, or economic maturity varies depending on the species, location, growing conditions, and intended use.

**Mature tree size**: Approximate size of a tree 40 years after planting.

**MBtu**: A unit of work or energy, measured as 1,000,000 British thermal units. One MBtu is equivalent to 0.293 MWh.

**Metric tonne (t)**: A measure of weight equal to 1,000,000 grams (1,000 kilograms) or 2,205 pounds.

**Municipal forester**: A person who manages public street and/or park trees (municipal forestry programs) for the benefit of the community.

**MWh (megawatt-hour)**: A unit of work or energy, measured as one megawatt (1,000,000 watts) of power expended for one hour. One MWh is equivalent to 3.412 Mbtu.

**Nitrogen oxides (oxides of nitrogen, NOx)**: A general term for compounds of nitric acid (NO), nitrogen dioxide ($NO_2$), and other oxides of nitrogen. Nitrogen oxides are typically created during combustion processes and are major contributors to smog formation and acid deposition. $NO_2$ may cause numerous adverse human health effects.

**Ozone**: A strong-smelling, pale blue, reactive toxic chemical gas consisting of three oxygen atoms. It is a product of the photochemical process involving the sun's energy. Ozone exists in the upper layer of the atmosphere as well as at the earth's surface. Ozone at the earth's surface can cause numerous adverse human health effects. It is a major component of smog.

**Peak cooling demand**: The greatest amount of electricity required at any one time during the course of a year to meet space cooling requirements.

**Peak flow (or peak runoff)**: The maximum rate of runoff at a given point or from a given area, during a specific period.

**Photosynthesis**: The process in green plants of converting water and carbon dioxide into sugar with light energy; accompanied by the production of oxygen.

**$PM_{10}$ (particulate matter)**: Major class of air pollutants consisting of tiny solid or liquid particles of soot, dust, smoke, fumes, and mists. The size of the particles (10 microns or smaller, about 0.0004 inches or less) allows them to enter the air sacs (gas-exchange region) deep in the lungs where they may be deposited and cause adverse health effects. $PM_{10}$ also reduces visibility.

**Resource unit (RU)**: The value used to determine and calculate benefits and costs of individual trees. For example, the amount of air conditioning energy saved in kWh/yr per tree, air-pollutant uptake in pounds per tree per year, or rainfall intercepted in gallons per tree per year.

**Riparian habitat**: Narrow strips of land bordering creeks, rivers, lakes, or other bodies of water.

**SEER (seasonal energy efficiency ratio)**: Ratio of cooling output to power consumption; kBtu-output/kWh-input as a fraction. It is the Btu of cooling output during normal annual usage divided by the total electric energy input in kilowatt-hours during the same period.

**Sequestration**: Annual net rate that a tree removes $CO_2$ from the atmosphere through the processes of photosynthesis and respiration (kg $CO_2$ per tree per year).

**Shade coefficient**: The percentage of light striking a tree crown that is transmitted through gaps in the crown. This is the percentage of light that hits the ground.

**Shade effects**: Impact on residential space heating and cooling (kg $CO_2$ per tree per year) from trees located within 50 ft (50 m) of a building.

**Solar-friendly trees**: Trees that have characteristics that reduce blocking of winter sunlight. According to one numerical ranking system, these traits include open crowns during the winter heating season, leaves that fall early and appear late, relatively small size, and a slow growth rate (Ames 1987).

**Sulfur dioxide ($SO_2$)**: A strong-smelling, colorless gas that is formed by the combustion of fossil fuels. Power plants, which may use coal or oil high in sulfur content, can be major sources of $SO_2$. Sulfur oxides contribute to the problem of acid deposition.

**Stem flow**: Amount of rainfall that travels down the tree trunk and onto the ground.

**Therm**: A unit of heat equal to 100,000 British thermal units (BTUs) or 100 kBtu. Also, 1 kBtu is equal to 0.01 therm.

**Throughfall**: Amount of rainfall that falls directly to the ground below the tree crown or drips onto the ground from branches and leaves.

**Transpiration**: The loss of water vapor through the stomata of leaves.

**Tree or canopy cover**: Within a specific area, the percentage covered by the crown of an individual tree or delimited by the vertical projection of its outermost perimeter; small openings in the crown are ignored. Used to express the relative importance of individual species within a vegetation community or to express the coverage of woody species.

**Tree litter**: Fruit, leaves, twigs, and other debris shed by trees.

**Tree-related emissions**: Carbon dioxide released when growing, planting, and caring for trees.

**Tree height**: Total height of tree from base (at groundline) to treetop.

**Tree-surface saturation storage (or tree-surface detention)**: The maximum volume of water that can be stored on a tree's leaves, stems and bark. This part of rainfall stored on the canopy surface does not contribute to surface runoff during and after a rainfall event.

**Urban heat island**: An area in a city where summertime air temperatures are 3 to 8°F warmer than temperatures in the surrounding countryside. Urban areas are warmer for two reasons: (1) Dark construction materials for roofs and asphalt that absorb solar energy, and (2) there are few trees, shrubs or other vegetation to provide shade and cool the air.

**VOCs (volatile organic compounds)**: Hydrocarbon compounds that exist in the ambient air. VOCs contribute to the formation of smog and/or are toxic. VOCs often have an odor. Some examples of VOCs are gasoline, alcohol, and the solvents used in paints.

**Willingness to pay**: The maximum amount of money an individual would be willing to pay, rather than do without, for non-market, public goods and services provided by environmental amenities such as trees and forests.

# *References*

**Akbari, H.; Davis, S.; Dorsano, S.; Huang, J.; Winnett, S., (Eds.). 1992.** Cooling Our Communities: A Guidebook on Tree Planting and Light-Colored Surfacing. Washington, DC: U.S. Environmental Protection Agency. 26 pp.

**American Forests. 1996.** Urban Ecological Analysis for Austin, Baltimore, Milwaukee. Washington, DC: American Forests. 32 pp.

**American Forests. 2002a.** Projected Benefits of Community Tree Planting: A Multi-Site Model Urban Forest Project in Atlanta. Washington, DC: American Forests. 12 pp.

**American Forests. 2002b.** Urban Ecological Analysis for the Washington DC Metropolitan Area. Washington, DC: American Forests. 16 pp.

**American Forests. 2002c.** Urban Ecological Analysis, Roanoke, Virginia. Washington, DC: American Forests. 8 pp.

**American Forests. 2003.** Urban Ecological Analysis, Mecklenburg County, North Carolina. Washington, DC: American Forests. 8 pp.

**American Forests. 2004.** Urban Ecological Analysis, Montgomery, AL. Washington, DC: American Forests. 12 pp.

**Ames, M.J. 1987.** Solar Friendly Trees Report. Portland, Oregon: City of Portland Energy Office.

**Anderson, L.M.; Cordell, H.K. 1988.** Residential property values improve by landscaping with trees. Southern Journal of Applied Forestry. 9:162–166.

**Benjamin, M.T.; Winer, A.M. 1998.** Estimating the ozone-forming potential of urban trees and shrubs. Atmos. Environ. 32:53–68.

**Bernhardt, E.; Swiecki, T.J. 1993.** The State of Urban Forestry in California: Results of the 1992 California Urban Forest Survey. Sacramento: California Department of Forestry and Fire Protection. 51 pp.

**Brenzel, K.N., (Ed.). 2001.** Sunset Western Garden Book. 7th ed. Menlo Park, CA: Sunset Books Inc.

**Cappiella, K.; Schueler, T.; Wright, T. 2005.** Urban Watershed Forestry Manual. Ellicot City, MD: Center for Watershed Protection.

**Chameides, W.L.; Lindsay, R.W.; Richardson, J.; Kiang, C.S. 1988.** The role of biogenic hydrocarbons in urban photochemical smog: Atlanta as a case study. Science. 241: 1473–1475.

**CO2e.com. 2005.** $CO_2$e Market Size and Pricing. Accessed via the World Wide Web <http://www.co2e.com/strategies/AdditionalInfo.asp?PageID=273#1613> on September 8, 2005.

**Cohen, J.E., Small, C., Mellinger, A., Gallup, J., and Sachs, J. 1997.** Estimates of coastal populations. Science. 278(5341):1211–1212.

**Cook, D.I. 1978.** Trees, solid barriers, and combinations: Alternatives for noise control. In: Proceedings of the National Urban Forestry Conference. ESF Pub. 80-003. Syracuse, NY: SUNY: 330–334.

**Costello, L.R. 2000.** Training Young Trees for Structure and Form. Videotape Number: V99-A. University of California, Agriculture and Natural Resources, Communication Services Cooperative Extension Service, Oakland, CA. (Telephone: 800-994-8849).

Costello, L.R.; Jones, K.S. 2003. Reducing Infrastructure Damage by Tree Roots: A Compendium of Strategies. Cohasset, CA: Western Chapter of the International Society of Arboriculture.

Duke Power. 2005. Accessed via the World Wide Web <http://www.dukepower.com/aboutus/rates/ncrates/> June 2005.

Dwyer, J.F.; McPherson, E.G.; Schroeder, H.W.; Rowntree, R.A. 1992. Assessing the benefits and costs of the urban forest. J. Arboric. 18(5):227–234.

Dwyer, M.C.; Miller, R.W. 1999. Using GIS to assess urban tree canopy benefits and surrounding greenspace distributions. J. Arboric. 25(2):102–107.

Fankhauser S. 1994. The social costs of greenhouse gas emissions: an expected value approach. The Energy Journal. 15: 157-184.

Gilman, E.F. 1997. Trees for Urban and Suburban Landscapes. Albany, NY: Delmar Publishing.

Gilman, E.F. 2002. An Illustrated Guide to Pruning. 2nd ed. Albany, NY: Delmar Publishing.

Gonzalez, S. 2004. Personal communication. Landscape Maintenance Manager, Vallejo, CA.

Guenther, A.B.; Monson, R.K.; Fall, R. 1991. Isoprene and monoterpene emission rate variability: observations with eucalyptus and emission rate algorithm development. Journal of Geophysical Research. 96:10799–10808.

Guenther, A.B.; Zimmermann, P.R.; Harley, P.C.; Monson, R.K.; Fall, R. 1993. Isoprene and monoterpene emission rate variability: model evaluations and sensitivity analyses. Journal of Geophysical Research. 98:12609–12617.

Hamburg, S.P.; Harris, N.; Jaeger, J.; Karl, T.R.; McFarland, M.; Mitchell, J.; Oppenheimer, M.; Santer, B.; Schneider, S.; Trenberth, K.; Wigley, T. 1997. Common questions about climate change. Nairobi, Kenya: United Nations Envirnment Programme, World Meteorological Organization. 22 pp.

Hammer, T.T.; Coughlin, R.; Horn, E. 1974. The effect of a large urban park on real estate value. Journal of the American Institute of Planning. July:274–275.

Hammond J.; Zanetto, J.; Adams, C. 1980. Planning Solar Neighborhoods. California Energy Commission.

Harris, R.W.; Clark, J.R.; Matheny, N.P. 1999. Arboriculture. 3rd ed. Englewood Cliffs, NJ: Regents/Prentice Hall.

Hartel, D. 2005. Personal communication. Center Coordinator, U.S. Department of Agriculture, Forest Service, Southern Research Station Headquarters, Asheville, NC.

Head, C.P.; Fisher, R.; O'Brien, M. 2001. Best Management Practices for Community Trees: A Technical Guide to Tree Conservation in Athens-Clarke County, Georgia. Athens, GA: Landscape Management Division Office.

Heisler, G.M. 1986. Energy savings with trees. J. Arboric. 12(5):113–125.

Hightshoe, G.L. 1988. Native Trees, Shrubs, and Vines for Urban and Rural America. New York: Van Nostrand Reinhold.

Hildebrandt, E.W.; Kallett, R.; Sarkovich, M.; Sequest, R. 1996. Maximizing the energy benefits of urban forestation. In: Proceedings of the ACEEE 1996 summer study on energy efficiency in buildings, volume 9; Washington DC: American Council for an Energy Efficient Economy: 121–131.

Hudson, B. 1983. Private sector business analogies applied in urban forestry. J. Arboric. 9(10):253–258.

**Hull, R.B. 1992.** How the public values urban forests. J. Arboric. 18(2):98–101.

**IPCC (Intergovernmental Panel on Climate Change). 2001.** Technical Summary. Climate Change 2001: The Scientific Basis. IPCC, Geneva. Accessed via the World Wide Web <http://www.ipcc.ch/pub/reports.htm> on December 19, 2005.

**ISA. 1992.** Avoiding tree and utility conflicts. Savoy, IL: International Society of Arboriculture. 4 pp.

**Jo, H.K.; McPherson, E.G. 1995.** Carbon storage and flux in residential greenspace. J. Environ. Manage. 45:109–133.

**Kaplan, R. 1992.** Urban Forestry and the Workplace. In: P.H. Gobster (Ed). Managing Urban and High-Use Recreation Settings. General Technical Report NC-163. Chicago, IL: U.S. Department of Agriculture, Forest Service, North Central Forest Experiment Station.

**Kaplan, R.; Kaplan, S. 1989.** The Experience of Nature: A Psychological Perspective. Cambridge, UK: Cambridge University Press.

**Karlik, J.F.; Winer, A.M. 2001.** Measured isoprene emission rates of plants in California landscapes: comparison to estimates from taxonomic relationships. Atmospheric Environment. 35:1123–1131.

**Lewis, C.A. 1996.** Green Nature/Human Nature: The Meaning of Plants in Our Lives. Chicago, IL: University of Illinois Press.

**Luley, C.J.; Bond, J. 2002.** A Plan to Integrate Management of Urban Trees into Air Quality Planning. Naples, NY: Davey Resource Group. 61 pp.

**Maco, S.E.; McPherson, E.G. 2003.** A practical approach to assessing structure, function, and value of street tree populations in small communities. J. Arboric. 29(2):84–97.

**Marion, W.; Urban, K. 1995.** User's Manual for TMY2s—Typical Meteorological Years. Golden, CO: National Renewable Energy Laboratory.

**Markwardt, L.J. 1930.** Comparative Strength Properties of Woods Grown in the United States. Tech. Bull. No. 158. Washington, DC: United States Department of Agriculture, Forest Service.

**McHale, M. 2003.** Carbon credit markets: Is there a role for community forestry? In: Kollin, C. (Ed.) 2003 National Urban Forest Conference Proceedings, San Antonio, TX. Washington, DC: American Forests: 74–77.

**McPherson, E.G. 1984.** Planting design for solar control. Chapter 8. In: Energy Conserving Site Design. Washington, DC: American Society of Landscape Architecture: 141-164.

**McPherson, E.G. 1992.** Accounting for benefits and costs of urban greenspace. Landscape and Urban Planning. 22: 41–51.

**McPherson, E.G. 1993.** Evaluating the cost effectiveness of shade trees for demand-side management. The Electricity Journal. 6(9):57–65.

**McPherson, E.G. 1994.** Energy-saving potential of trees in Chicago. In: McPherson, E.G., Nowak, D.J., Rowntree, R.A. (Eds.). Chicago's Urban Forest Ecosystem: Results of the Chicago Urban Forest Climate Project. GTR NE-186. Radnor, PA: U.S. Department of Agriculture, Forest Service, Northeastern Forest Experiment Station: 95–113.

**McPherson, E.G. 1995.** Net benefits of healthy and productive forests. In: Bradley, G.A. (Ed.). 1995. Urban forest landscapes: Integrating multidisciplinary perspectives. Seattle, WA: University of Washington Press: 180–194.

**McPherson, E.G. 1997.** Airing it out. Davis, CA : Spring Update, Center for Urban Forest Research, U.S. Department of Agriculture, Forest Service, Pacific Southwest Research Station. 4 pp.

**McPherson, E.G. 1998.** Atmospheric carbon dioxide reduction by Sacramento's urban forest. J. Arboric. 24(4):215–223.

**McPherson, E.G. 2000.** Expenditures associated with conflicts between street tree root growth and hardscape in California. J. Arboric. 26(6):289–297.

**McPherson, E.G. 2001.** Sacramento's parking lot shading ordinance: environmental and economic costs of compliance. Landscape and Urban Planning. 57:105–123.

**McPherson, E.G.; Mathis, S. (Eds.) 1999.** Proceedings of the Best of the West Summit. Sacramento, CA: Western Chapter, International Society of Arboriculture. 93 pp.

**McPherson, E.G., J. Muchnick. 2005.** Effects of street tree shade on asphalt concrete pavement performance. Journal of Arboriculture. 31(6):303-310

**McPherson, E.G.; Peper, P.J. 1995.** Infrastructure repair costs associated with street trees in 15 cities. In: Watson, G.W.; Neely, D. (Eds.). Trees and Building Sites. Champaign, IL: International Society of Arboriculture: 49–63.

**McPherson, E.G.; Simpson, J.R. 1999.** Guidelines for Calculating Carbon Dioxide Reductions Through Urban Forestry Programs. PSW-GTR-171. Albany, CA: U.S. Department of Agriculture, Forest Service, Pacific Southwest Research Station.

**McPherson, E.G.; Simpson, J.R. 2003.** Potential energy savings in buildings by an urban tree planting programme in California. Urban For. Urban Green. 2:73–86.

**McPherson, E.G.; Sacamano, P.L.; Wensman, S. 1993.** Modeling Benefits and Costs of Community Tree Plantings. Davis, CA: U.S. Department of Agriculture, Forest Service, Pacific Southwest Research Station. 170 pp.

**McPherson, E.G.; Nowak, D.J.; Rowntree, R.A. 1994.** Chicago's Urban Forest Ecosystem: Results of the Chicago Urban Forest Climate Project. Gen. Tech. Rep. NE-186. Radnor, PA: U.S. Department of Agriculture, Forest Service, Northeastern Forest Experiment Station. 201 p.

**McPherson, E.G.; Simpson, J.R.; Peper, P.J.; Xiao, Q. 1999a.** Tree Guidelines for San Joaquin Valley Communities. Sacramento, CA: Local Government Commission. 63 pp.

**McPherson, E.G.; Simpson, J.R.; Peper, P.J.; Xiao, Q. 1999b.** Benefit-cost analysis of Modesto's municipal urban forest. J. Arboric. 25(5):235–248.

**McPherson, E.G.; Simpson, J.R.; Peper, P.J.; Scott, K.; Xiao, Q. 2000.** Tree Guidelines for Coastal Southern California Communities. Sacramento, CA: Local Government Commission. 97 pp.

**McPherson, E.G.; Simpson, J.R.; Peper, P.J.; Maco, S.E.; Xiao, Q.; Hoefer, P.J. 2003.** Northern Mountain and Prairie Community Tree Guide: Benefits, Costs, and Strategic Planting. Davis, CA: Center for Urban Forest Research, U.S. Department of Agriculture, Forest Service.

**McPherson, E.G.; Simpson, J.R.; Peper, P.J.; Maco, S.E.; Gardner, S.L.; Cozad, S.K.; Xiao, Q. 2005a.** Midwest Community Tree Guide: Benefits, Costs, and Strategic Planting. NA-TP-05-05. Newton Square, PA: Northeastern Area State and Private Forestry, U.S. Department of Agriculture, Forest Service.

**McPherson, E.G.; Simpson, J.R.; Peper, P.J.; Gardner, S.L.; Vargas, K.E.; Ho, J.; Maco, S.; Xiao, Q. 2005b.** City of Charlotte, North Carolina, Municipal Forest Resource Analysis. Internal Tech. Rep. Davis, CA: U.S. Department of Agriculture, Forest Service, Pacific Southwest Research Station.

**Metro. 2002.** Green Streets: Innovative Solutions for Stormwater and Stream Crossings. Portland, OR: Metro.

**Metropolitan Council. 2004.** Twin Cities Area Population. Accessed via the World Wide Web <http://www.metrocouncil.org/about/facts/TwinCitiesPopulationFacts.pdf> on Dec 12, 2004.

Miller, R.W. 1997. Urban Forestry: Planning and Managing Urban Greenspaces. 2[d] edn. Upper Saddle River, NJ: Prentice-Hall. 502 pp.

More, T.A.; Stevens, T; Allen, P.G. 1988. Valuation of urban parks. Landscape and Urban Planning. 15:139–52.

Natural Resource Conservation Service (NRCS), Agroforestry Center. 2005. Working trees for treating waste. Western Arborist. 31:50-52.

Neely, D. (Ed.) 1988. Valuation of Landscape Trees, Shrubs, and Other Plants. 7th ed. Urbana, IL: International Society of Arboriculture. 50 pp.

Noble, R.D.; Martin, J.L.; Jensen, K.F. 1988. Air pollution effects on vegetation, including forest ecosystems. Proceedings of the Second US-USSR Symposium, Corvallis, OR, 1988. Gov. Doc. A13.42/2:2:A:7. Broomall, PA: U.S. Department of Agriculture, Forest Service, Northeastern Forest Experiment Station.

Nowak, D.J. 1994a. Atmospheric carbon dioxide reduction by Chicago's urban forest. In: McPherson, E.G., Nowak, D.J., Rowntree, R.A. (Eds.). Chicago's Urban Forest Ecosystem: Results of the Chicago Urban Forest Climate Project. GTR NE-186, Radnor, PA: U.S. Department of Agriculture, Forest Service, Northeastern Forest Experiment Station: 83-94.

Nowak, D.J. 1994b. Air pollution removal by Chicago's urban forest. In: McPherson, E.G., Nowak, D.J., Rowntree, R.A. (Eds.) Chicago's Urban Forest Ecosystem: Results of the Chicago Urban Forest Climate Project. GTR NE-186, Radnor, PA: U.S. Department of Agriculture, Forest Service, Northeastern Forest Experiment Station: 63–82.

Nowak, D.J. 2000. Tree species selection, design, and management to improve air quality. In: Scheu, D.L. (Ed.) 2000 ASLA Annual Meeting Proceedings, St. Louis, MO. Washington DC: American Society of Landscape Architects: 23–27.

Nowak, D.J.; Crane, D.E. 2002. Carbon storage and sequestration by urban trees in the USA. Environmental Pollution. 116:381–389.

Nowak, D.J., Civerolo, K.L.; Rao, S.T., Sistla, G.; Luley, C.J.; Crane, D.E. 2000. A modeling study of the impact of urban trees on ozone. Atmospheric Environment. 34:1601–1613.

Ottinger, R.L.; Wooley, D.R.; Robinson, N.A.; Hodas, D.R.; Babb, S.E. 1990. Environmental Costs of Electricity. New York: Pace University Center for Environmental Legal Studies, Oceana Publications.

Parsons, R.; Tassinary, L.G.; Ulrich, R.S.; Hebl, M.R.; Grossman-Alexander, M. 1998. The view from the road: implications for stress recovery and immunization. Journal of Environmental Psychology. 18(2):113–140.

Peper, P.J.; McPherson, E.G. 2003. Evaluation of four methods for estimating leaf area of isolated trees. Urban For. Urban Green. 2:19–29.

Piedmont Natural Gas 2004. Accessed via the World Wide Web <http://www.piedmontng.com/rates/ratesNC?pageId=092004NC.htm&section=res> June 2005.

Pillsbury, N.H.; Reimer, J.L.; Thompson R.P. 1998. Tree Volume Equations for Fifteen Urban Species in California. Tech. Rep. 7. San Luis Obispo, CA: Urban Forest Ecosystems Institute, California Polytechnic State University. 56 pp.

Platt, R.H.; Rowntree, R.A.; Muick, P.C., (Eds). 1994. The Ecological City. Boston, MA: University of Massachusetts. 292 pp.

Ramsay, S. 2002. Personal communication on December 19, 2002. Executive Director, Trees Forever, Marion, IA.

Richards, N.A.; Mallette, J.R.; Simpson, R.J.; Macie, E.A. 1984. Residential greenspace and vegetation in a mature city: Syracuse, New York. Urban Ecol. 8:99–125.

Sand, M. 1991. Planting for energy conservation in the north. Minneapolis, MN: Minnesota Department of Natural Resources. 19 pp.

Sand, M. 1993. Energy conservation through community forestry. St. Paul: University of Minnesota. 40 pp.

Sand, M. 1994. Design and species selection to reduce urban heat island and conserve energy. In: Proceedings from the Sixth National Urban Forest Conference: Growing Greener Communities. Washington DC: American Forests: 282.

Schroeder, T. 1982. The relationship of local park and recreation services to residential property values. Journal of Leisure Research. 14:223–234.

Schroeder, H.W.; Cannon, W.N. 1983. The esthetic contribution of trees to residential streets in Ohio towns. J. Arboric. 9:237–243.

Scott, K.I.; McPherson, E.G.; Simpson, J.R. 1998. Air pollutant uptake by Sacramento's urban forest. J. Arboric. 24(4):224–234.

Scott, K.I.; Simpson, J.R.; McPherson, E.G. 1999. Effects of tree cover on parking lot microclimate and vehicle emissions. J. Arboric. 25(3):129–142.

Simpson, J.R. 1998. Urban forest impacts on regional space conditioning energy use: Sacramento County case study. J. Arboric. 24(4):201–214.

Smith, W.H. 1990. Air pollution and forests. New York: Springer-Verlag. 618 pp.

Smith, W.H.; Dochinger, L.S. 1976. Capability of metropolitan trees to reduce atmospheric contaminants. In: Santamour, F.S., Gerhold, H.D., Little, S. (Eds.) Better Trees for Metropolitan Landscapes. GTR NE-22. Upper Darby, PA. U.S. Department of Agriculture, Forest Service: 49–60.

Sullivan, W.C.; Kuo, E.E. 1996. Do trees strengthen urban communities, reduce domestic violence? Arborist News. 5(2):33–34.

Summit, J.; McPherson, E.G. 1998. Residential tree planting and care: a study of attitudes and behavior in Sacramento, California. J. Arboric. 24(2):89–97.

Sydnor, T.D.; Gamstetter, D.; Nichols, J.; Bishop, B.; Favorite, J.; Blazer, C.; Turpin, L. 2000. Trees are not the root of sidewalk problems. J.Arboric. 26:20–29.

Taha, H. 1996. Modeling impacts of increased urban vegetation on ozone air quality in the South Coast Air Basin. Atmospheric Environment. 30:3423–3420.

Thompson, R.P.; Ahern, J.J. 2000. The State of Urban and Community Forestry in California. San Luis Obispo, CA: Urban Forest Ecosystems Institute, California Polytechnic State University.

Tretheway, R.; Manthe, A. 1999. Skin cancer prevention: another good reason to plant trees. In: McPherson, E.G., Mathis, S. (Eds.) Proceedings of the Best of the West Summit. Davis, CA: University of California, Davis: 72–75.

Tschantz, B.A.; Sacamano, P.L. 1994. Municipal Tree Management in the United States. Kent, OH: Davey Resource Group.

Tyrvainen, L. 1999. Monetary Valuation of Urban Forest Amenities in Finland. Research Paper 739. Vantaa, Finland: Finnish Forest Research Institute. 129 pp.

Ulrich, R.S. 1985. Human responses to vegetation and landscapes. Landscape and Urban Planning. 13:29-44.

Urban, J. 1992. Bringing order to the technical dysfunction within the urban forest. J. Arboric. 18(2):85-90.

US Census Bureau. 2002. State and County Quick Facts. Accessed via the World Wide Web <http://quickfacts.census.gov/qfd/states/08/08001.html> in June 2005.

US EPA (U.S. Environmental Protection Agency). 1998. Ap-42 Compilation of Air Pollutant Emission Factors (5th ed). Volume I. Research Triangle Park, NC.

US EPA. 2003. E-GRID (E-GRID2002 Edition). Accessed via the World Wide Web <http://www.epa.gov/cleanenergy/egrid/index.htm> on June 2, 2004.

US EPA. 2005. Green book: nonattainment areas for criteria pollutants. Accessed via the World Wide Web <http://www.epa.gov/oar/oaqps/greenbk/index.html> on May 2, 2005.

Wang, M.Q.; Santini, D.J. 1995. Monetary values of air pollutant emissions in various U.S. regions. Transportation Research Record. 1475:33–41.

Watson, G.W.; Himelick, E.B. 1997. Principles and practice of planting trees and shrubs. Savoy, IL: International Society of Arboriculture. 199 pp.

Winer, A.M.; Karlik, J.; Arey, J.;Chung, Y.J.; A. Reissell. 1998. Biogenic Hydrocarbon Inventories for California: Generation of Essential Databases. Final Report Contract No. 95. Los Angeles, CA: California Air Resources Board. 309 pp.

Wolf, K.L., 1999. Nature and commerce: human ecology in business districts. In: Kollin, C. (Ed.). Building Cities of Green: Proceedings of the 1999 National Urban Forest Conference. Washington, DC: American Forests: 56–59.

Xiao, Q.; McPherson, E.G.; Simpson, J.R.; Ustin, S.L. 1998. Rainfall interception by Sacramento's urban forest. J. Arboric. 24(4):235–244.

Xiao, Q.; McPherson, E.G.; Simpson, J.R.; Ustin, S.L. 2000. Winter rainfall interception by two mature open grown trees in Davis, California. Hydrological Processes. 14(4):763–784.

Xiao, Q.; McPherson, E.G. 2002. Rainfall interception by Santa Monica's municipal urban forest. Urban Ecosystems. 6:291–302.

www.ingramcontent.com/pod-product-compliance
Lightning Source LLC
Chambersburg PA
CBHW080317290526
45790CB00005B/2071